**DO NOT REMOVE
CARDS FROM POCKET**

EXPLORING CAREERS IN NURSING

EXPLORING CAREERS IN NURSING

by

Jackie Heron, RN

THE ROSEN PUBLISHING GROUP, INC.
New York

Published in 1986, 1988 by Rosen Publishing Group, Inc.
29 East 21st Street, New York, NY 10010

Revised Edition 1988
Copyright 1986, 1988 by Jackie Heron, RN

Library of Congress Cataloging in Publication Data

Heron, Jackie.
  Exploring careers in nursing.

  (Exploring careers)
  Includes index.
  I. Nursing—Vocational guidance—Juvenile literature.
I. Title. II. Series: Exploring careers (Rosen
Publishing Group) [DNLM: 1. Careers Choice. 2. Nursing.
WY 16 H562e]
RT82.H47 1986 610.73'023   86-13066
ISBN 0-8239-0799-6

Manufactured in the United States of America

Acknowledgments

I would like to thank the nurses who responded to my Successful Nurse's Questionnaire. Their contributions greatly enhanced the realistic scope of information presented. In alphabetical order: Chris Bekish, Pam Emmons, Stacy Schoendorf, Pamela Schuman, Vera Shy, Carlene Smith, Deborah Truitt, and Larry Vander Meulen.

A special note of thanks to Ruth Rosen, my editor, for her guidance and suggestions.

A big thank-you to Renee Dunham, my word processor. Without Renee's services, this book would probably still be in handwritten form.

A personal thank-you to my husband, Ross Heron, for his loving encouragement and support.

Introduction

This book is written to acquaint you with the world of nursing. The contents are designed to be informative, thought-provoking, and educationally entertaining. A variety of charts, situational questions, and illustrations, when used in conjunction with the text, will help you to achieve valuable self-awareness. Properly applied, the data should enable you to determine your degree of compatibility with the nursing profession.

Contents

EXPLORING CAREERS IN NURSING

Chapter **1**

Welcome to the World of Nursing!

The world of nursing is fascinating, progressive, challenging, and refreshingly versatile. Nursing is a people-oriented profession: human beings helping other human beings to reach their optimum health potential. The nurse's commitment to another person's physical, mental, psychological, and emotional well-being requires complete professional involvement. On one side, a nurse's selfless professional dedication presents endless challenges, sacrifices, and demands for the nurse to cope with. On the other side, the satisfaction nursing brings to a professional nurse is total.

Nursing is unlike many other professions in that automation and robotics technology cannot threaten a professional nurse's job security. Mechanical devices are incapable of reproducing and displaying spontaneous human responses. Your empathic and compassionate response to the patient, in conjunction with evaluation of the patient's subjective complaints and covert signs and symptoms of illness, could mean the difference between optimum health or recurring illness. Therefore, the essence of nursing is human input and human feedback.

Even though the writing of this book is not a direct patient-care task, the function consists of human input and human feedback. The author, a professional nurse, is describing the intricacies of the nursing profession to help you, the reader, determine your compatibility with that profession.

How will the "facts of life for the professional nurse" affect you? This could be your life!

Facts of Life for the Professional Nurse

All professions offer their share of frustrations and problems, nursing being no exception. Whether an issue becomes a problem, a frustration, or an accepted and tolerated aspect of nursing depends on how you perceive each idiosyncrasy and the coping mechanisms you elect to employ. Most nurses feel that they can deal effectively with the frustrations and problems. Successful nurses see their profession's idiosyncrasies as facts of life. Even when self-sacrifice is deemed necessary, the nurse's personal loss is greatly buffered by the personal satisfaction derived from helping others to meet their holistic health needs.

As you review the following facts of life for the professional nurse, decide to what degree each one would affect your life-style and how you could adapt.

Remember, your basic personality qualities of flexibility, compromise, adaptability, and self-sacrifice play a significant role in the fact-finding process. As you draw your final conclusion, be honest with yourself. If nursing is your profession, you will know.

The following aspects of nursing generally pertain to nurses giving direct patient care. However, each could probably be found in other fields of nursing. How would you react to the following facts of life as a nurse?

- Would they pose a few minor inconveniences to which you could readily adjust?
- Would they present major problems that you would voluntarily make adaptations to accommodate?
- Would the changes in your life-style be so drastic as to be inconceivable?

1. Your time is not always your own.

How important are your social life, your family, and your free time? Would it bother you to work hours other than 9:00 a.m. to 5:00 p.m. and days other than Monday through Friday?

Nurses usually work three shifts to cover a patient's needs on a 24-hour basis. The eight-hour shift is the most common, although modifications are made to meet the requirements of the nurse and the health-care organization.

Usually, the first shift is days, and you work from 7:00 a.m. to 3:30 p.m. If your tour of duty commences at 3:00 p.m. and ends at 11:30, you are a second-shift or afternoon nurse. If you begin at 11:00 p.m. and go off duty at 7:30 a.m., you are a midnight or third-shift nurse. All three shifts have their advantages and disadvantages.

- Could you tolerate having different days off each week, or one day off at a time? Sometimes that is the way you are scheduled.
- What is your opinion of every other weekend off? This is common practice in most situations.
- Would you resent working on Christmas or other holidays? As a rule, you will be scheduled on duty every other holiday unless you switch with a co-worker.
- Could you withstand the stress of rotating shifts? Although not a common practice anymore, it still happens.
- Would you bristle at permanent placement on any particular shift? Sometimes your preference may not be possible.
- Does working overtime, on your day off, or on a double shift present a hardship?
- Would you be willing to work "on call"? You must be available to come in on your day off if the need arises. You may be asked to take "on call" on a routine basis, during staff shortages, or for emergencies only.

Scheduling considerations affect most nurses to some degree; but, naturally, there are exceptions. Not all nurses are required to work odd shifts and days, but many do for a lifetime. Patients do not have automatic controls to be sick only between 9:00 a.m. and 5:00 p.m. Monday through Friday, with weekends and holidays off. Inevitably, your work schedule will interfere with your domestic and social life. How would you adapt to the restrictions?

Nursing is your life-style. For you to succeed, your family must understand and accept your career goals and be willing to encourage and support your efforts to achieve them. Compatibility between the two worlds, coupled with personal satisfaction, is the ultimate accomplishment. Effective time management, advance planning, organizational skill, adaptability, flexibility, and ability to compromise can eliminate most major conflicts.

2. Nursing challenges and tests your human relations skills.

Can you read and follow directions and take verbal orders without mistakes? Physicians' orders are the substance of patient care. Your nursing care plan is developed from the doctor's orders. An incorrectly performed or neglected doctor's order could kill a patient. The importance of being able to read and precisely follow a physician's order cannot be overstated. The physician may discuss with you and incorporate your professional suggestions into the orders. Nevertheless, in a court of law and to the health governing agencies, the physician's orders are legally binding. The bottom line is whether you can read and flawlessly follow directions.

Do you function well as a team member? Primary nursing on a hospital unit constitutes a one-to-one nurse-patient ratio; but unless you are the only health care professional responsible for a patient, you will be part of a therapeutic team. As a team member, you will be expected to consult with fellow members on a patient's condition, contribute information during patient-care conferences, and meet specific team obligations.

How do you react to personality conflicts? Whenever you work with other people, you face the possibility of a personality clash. Can you remain nonjudgmental, maintaining your poise and composure? Are you capable of completing your assignment without adverse effects on your patient care? Are you able to sit down with the "enemy" and rationally negotiate a compromise? Are you capable of waiting for an appropriate time, place, and approach to resolve personal animosities without involving patients?

3. Are you and your conscience good friends?

How do you handle moral and ethical issues? Nursing has many issues that, if not carefully analyzed and evaluated, could victimize an innocent someone. Sometimes there are no right or wrong answers. Other answers are painstakingly difficult to find because your values strongly influence your reactions. Here is a real case history with fictional names to demonstrate the point.

You are a staff nurse on an Orthopedic Unit. Patients on this unit frequently have broken bones and require pain medication regularly. A narcotic is often the drug of choice to alleviate pain.

The nurse under scrutiny is also a staff nurse on your shift. Carol Kay is a "model" nurse, proficient at technical nursing skills, respected by physicians, loved by patients, and very knowledgeable in Orthopedic Nursing.

For four nights you have covered Carol's patients during her lunch and coffee breaks. Each night Harold Evans, the patient in Room 522, has complained of excruciating pain around 5:00 p.m.

COURTESY WILLIAM BEAUMONT HOSPITAL
An RN provides inservice training.

You check the patient's chart to see when he was last medicated for pain. Carol's charting indicates that she medicated the patient with Demerol 100 mg I.M. (intramuscular injection) at 5:00 p.m. on the first night, 4:55 p.m. the second evening, and 5:00 p.m. the third night. The consistency of his complaints of severe pain prompts you to check his chart. You note that his only complaints of pain are on the afternoon shift.

At 9:00 p.m. you are giving h.s. (bedtime) care, and in passing by you notice that Carol's medication cart is unlocked. You stop to lock the cart and notice that the medication book is open to

Harold's sheet. You see the curtain pulled and hear Carol talking with the patient. Assuming that she forgot to lock her cart, you continue with your rounds. On your return trip, Carol stops you to ask for help in pulling Harold up in bed. You notice a tubex and butterfly I.V. (intravenous) setup in her pocket. In the patient's room, you see an empty, plain syringe and needle on the bedside table. Could Carol be taking the Demerol and injecting the patient with sterile sodium chloride?

On the fourth night Harold's dilemma prompts you to take action. This situation gives you the opportunity to explore your ethical and moral values and make some judgments. What would you do?

A. Ignore the entire incident. It is none of your business. Carol is a close social friend of yours. Besides, if Carol is guilty, you could be drawn into a legal hassle. If you falsely accuse her, she could sue you for defamation of character. Least of all, you could conceivably lose a real friend.

B. Explain to Harold that it is too soon to repeat his pain medication. Ask open-ended questions to determine whether activity or time of day could be a factor. Offer him a back rub, and institute other nursing comfort measures. Tell him to call you in an hour if he still has no relief, and that you will then call his physician. Accurately document all pertinent data. Report the facts to his primary nurse, Carol, when she returns from her break.

C. Confidentially discuss the problem with your immediate supervisor, mentioning the full tubex you saw in Carol's pocket. Carrying a federally regulated drug in your pocket is not good nursing practice.

D. During your coffee break, ease your conscience by sharing your burden with mutual friends and seeking their opinion.

E. Confide in Dr. Ross, Harold's private physician and chief of staff. You have worked closely with him during several controversial, confidential interdepartmental disputes.

F. Confront Carol with your observations to classify your suspicions as fact or fiction.

G. Unobtrusively observe and evaluate Carol for drug-related changes in her physical, psychological, mental, or emotional status. At the first signs of drug abuse, report her directly to the authorities.

Several of the above responses are correct when tactfully and appropriately executed. The hidden variables are the elements that make a response appropriate or inappropriate. As you study the author's analysis, draw your own conclusions in accordance with your ethical and moral values.

Remember these important criteria as you make your responses. Your professionalism will be tested to the limit in this situation. You must be especially adept at making accurate observations with comprehensive, detailed documentation. Be sure that all actions you take are morally, ethically, and professionally sound. Preserve your reputation, Carol's, and the unit's by using discretion, diplomacy, and confidentiality. Take the necessary legal and professional precautions to prevent violation of everyone's rights.

If you said, A, D, and E were the *least* appropriate responses, you were correct. A patient is in pain, and you are one of the nurses responsible for his care during the time in question. Therefore, you are legally accountable for your actions. Friendship does not separate right from wrong. Your concern for the patient's well-being still takes precedence. Even if you remain silent and aloof, you could still be drawn into a legal battle. Accurate documentation of the facts and discretion are your best means to avert a lawsuit, particularly if the main subject is the patient's uncontrolled pain.

The first step to take is B. To save yourself possible grief, it is imperative that your documentation be detailed and accurate, whether it is a routine procedure or a questionable incident. If you are called into court seven years from now, will you vividly recall the details? If it is in writing, it will be easy to refresh your memory.

Step two could conceivably be C. Show your supervisor your documentation on the patient's chart. Next, give your superior a detailed written report, including dates, times, specifics of the four nights in question, and the actions taken by you. Do not forget to include significant facts such as that on Carol's days off the patient did not complain of pain after his early-afternoon Demerol injection. Remember, these are facts, *not* opinions, and they should be unbiased and nonjudgmental. Sign and date your information. Make a photostatic copy for yourself and file it in a safe place (preferably at home). Give the original to the proper authority.

Action A is definitely incorrect. A patient is being neglected, and you are one of his nurses. If you fail to record and report the facts, you are legally liable.

If you chose action D at all, it should have been with many qualifications and some reservations. There is no need to involve a third party, unless that person has the knowledge and authority to decide the issue. Further, if your coffee break is off the unit, you run the risk of violating everyone's confidentiality. Talking with mutual friends about a potentially explosive problem is in poor taste. In addition, there is a fine line between gossiping and helping a friend, especially when the friend in question is unaware of the conversation.

Choice E is the only aspect, if any, that you should report to the physician. If the patient is in jeopardy, the attending physician should be notified. There could be an important reason for Harold's analgesic to be ineffective at that hour of the day. There is no reason to mention Carol to the doctor, because you have only circumstantial evidence.

Some people firmly believe that F is step one. However, unless you possess exceptional interpersonal skills, you would be wise to leave that to someone more detached from, and able to control the outcome of, the situation. If Carol is innocent and you handle yourself badly, you have made an enemy, and perhaps other nurses will resent your "attitude." If Carol is guilty and you fail to follow the complex legal process properly, you could be named an accessory to a crime. Proceed with caution if this is your choice.

G is a mediocre response. You should, if time permits, make a few observations before reporting Carol to your supervisor. However, if you are doing your job, you are usually too busy to plan strategic observation. That might better be left in the hands of the powers-that-be.

Why all the fuss about moral and ethical issues? They are an integral part of the nurse's thought process. Granted, not all of them are as powerful or obvious as this one, but none comes without consequences for all persons involved. They are judgments that originate in your conscience, and therefore are not easily made. To add to the complexity, one must remember that the end result could have devastating and irreversible effects on others.

Have you drawn your conclusions as to whether the nurse was guilty or not guilty? Here is the real truth.

The tubex injector had been defective, and Carol had used a regular syringe to draw up and administer the Demerol to the patient. The sodium chloride in her hand was used to mix another patient's I.V. feeding. In her haste to respond to an emergency, she put the defective tubex in her pocket, intending to report the problem to the tubex manufacturer's representative. If you falsely accused her of drug abuse, where would that leave you?

Here is another moral-ethical issue to ponder. As you think about this one, consider your personal involvement in the work environment and how these problems would affect you. The first one you could have easily ignored; this one you cannot run from. You are the patient's nurse, and you are in the spotlight. What would you do to help this woman?

A 37-year-old female has just been diagnosed metastatic Ca (cancer) of the brain, an inoperable tumor with a poor prognosis. She has approximately six months to live. Her husband has conferred with the physician and requested that his wife *not* be informed that she is dying. While you are caring for her, she asks you if she is dying. What would you say?

A. I am not allowed to discuss your illness with you.
B. Everything will be fine; just let us take care of you.
C. How did you find out you were dying?

Answer A greatly reduces your credibility with the patient, implying that you know something she does not and will not share the information with her.

Answer B is a deliberate lie, and grossly unfair to the patient.

Answer C is also wrong. You have disobeyed the doctor's orders.

What is the right answer? Ask open-ended questions to determine how much knowledge versus intuition comprised her question. Collect the facts and present them to the physician. If that does not yield results, set up an appointment to discuss the situation with the physician, the nursing supervisor, and the husband. Perhaps request a patient-care conference among the entire interdisciplinary team.

4. Confidentiality is mandatory for success in nursing.

Common sense tells you what information should be discreetly revealed, when, and to whom. If you are uncertain, ask your immediate supervisor for advice.

5. "Other people first" often becomes a way of life.

Do you care enough about strangers to feel the pain another feels? Can you put yourself in the patients' place and understand their anxieties, frustrations, and fears? Many nurses are dedicated people working long hours and putting forth extra energy to help those in need find answers to pressing problems. Their dedication can give them a tendency to become emotionally, mentally, and psychologically involved with patients, which can cause a multitude of problems for the nurse. If a patient's problem cannot be solved immediately, the urge to discuss or think out the problem at home can be very strong. Consequently, the nurse's frustration adversely affects the equilibrium of her family or social life. At times, the high stress created by added responsibilities at work is compounded by the inability to solve a work problem without a constructive release at home. Family and friends may have difficulty empathizing with your problem. Only you can set your guidelines for contentment based on your personal and professional circumstances.

Yesterday's, Today's, and Tomorrow's Nurses

As you consider the nursing profession, you probably wonder who today's nurses are. Where are they employed? What are their responsibilities? What clothes do they wear? What hours do they work?

What mental image do you create when you think of a nurse? A female between the ages of eighteen and sixty-five, wearing a white uniform, white hose, sparkling white oxfords, a nurse's cap, name pin, and school pin. The bulge in her front pocket conceals a pen, a pad of paper, a pen light, and her patient assignment sheet. Protruding above her left pocket is a pair of bandage scissors and a hemostat. To complete the picture, a stethoscope may dangle around her neck. That image has its merits, but also its fallacies.

Today's nurses are both male and female. Even though nursing remains predominantly female, increasing numbers of males are assuming roles as professional nurses.

Age is not a dominating factor. Many fields of nursing can be modified to meet specific needs of the senior nurse.

Your work wardrobe allows ample individual and personality expression. You have a wide selection of colors, materials, patterns, and styles to meet your personal preference while satisfying professional requirements. You may choose from culottes, pants suits, scrubs, and even street clothes in some fields of nursing. Drab olive green scrubs are largely obsolete. Lively, cheerful colors and styles adorn many of today's nurses. Fashions for both men and women are available at retail stores. The dreaded prickly, starched garment has yielded to a softer, more natural permanent-press fabric. Cotton, because of its practicality, durability, and versatility, remains popular, although it shares its domain with many other choices. White hose are optional in some situations, yet preferred by many female nurses and viewed as a status symbol. Nursing caps are fading into the past in some domains but are part of the dress code in other places. Lots of nurses still wear their school nursing pin close to their heart; but, for the most part, employers do not require it. Stethoscopes are usually supplied by the hospital, but many nurses purchase their own.

Where will you find nurses? Hospitals are common gathering grounds. After that, nurses disperse and can be found in nursing homes, in factories as occupational nurses, in private homes, in government agencies and schools, in their own offices as consultants, in mental and general health clinics, in physicians' offices, and in health clubs and weight loss clinics.

Even though health care delivery systems are experiencing major changes, hospitals still employ a vast majority of this country's nurses. For the benefit of anyone who has never been in a hospital, let us take a grand tour of a typical acute-care hospital.

As you enter the front door, you will be standing in the lobby. You will see a comfortable seating arrangement for visitors and perhaps a television set. As you proceed, you may pass the chapel, the front office, and the gift shop. Nearby you will find the information desk, which performs multiple functions; the best known is issuing visitors' passes to see patients. From there, your next stop will be the elevators that provide transportation to the separate patient units.

The hospital is divided into several floors. In turn, each floor is subdivided into many rooms, primarily private and semiprivate. Each room houses a human being with a particular illness. Patients with a certain kind of ailment are usually grouped together on the same floor. At a glance, you will see that a busy patient unit is bustling with health care professionals and hospital staff. These include physicians, nursing personnel, pharmacist, X-ray technicians, laboratory technicians, dietary staff, laundry employees, maintenance men, housekeepers, and staff from numerous other departments such as medical records, infection control, or risk management. The corridors are often long, with only an incidental break in the straight lines: someone's medication cart. A call light is above each room door. Often a community tub and shower is shared by several patients. The patients are frequently dressed in garb lovingly called patient gowns. All cotton, one size fits all, one style to choose from—white with blue print. Hospital linen is usually cotton, usually white, with standard thermal bedspreads. The towels—you guessed it—as a rule are one color, one size. That is beginning to change, but slowly.

Upon entering a private or semiprivate patient room, you might see a wall TV with remote control. This can be rented for a small fee, on a daily or weekly basis, if the patient's condition permits. There is usually one bathroom per room. That cord you see by the toilet, when pulled, lights a red light above the room door, activating a shrill alarm to alert staff that a patient needs help immediately. Patients use their own toiletries. Beds are fingertip control and can assume many positions to accommodate patients' therapeutic and comfort needs. The nurses' call light is attached at the wall outlet and lying on the bed, or is an integrated part of the bed controls. When the call light button is pushed at the bedside, the corresponding light above the door outside the room lights up. That is the nurses' signal that assistance is needed.

The nurses' station and conference room provide nursing staff a place to make phone calls, pick up medications, leave specimens, and have conferences. When a shift is over, nurses usually leave by the employee exit, which bypasses the mainstream of people and equipment traffic. It provides easy access to the nurses' locker room, the employee cafeteria, and the time clock, plus other employee-designated areas.

Now that you have toured the hospital, it is time to go to work. A typical day in the life of a hospital nurse begins as your alarm clock bleeps its final warning. A new day is calling you. Burdened with worry about a critically ill patient, you bounce out of bed, scramble through a shower, dress appropriately, and prepare for a physically and mentally challenging day at work. On the way you might draw a mental image of your tour of duty.

You arrive at your place of employment at 6:30 a.m., clock in, go to your locker, and organize your personal effects. Your next stop is the cafeteria for juice and a muffin. You reach your assigned unit at 6:45 a.m. You make general assessment rounds as you await your assignment for this tour of duty, unless you already know your assignment. Does it look as if midnights went smoothly, or was there an emergency that disrupted everyone's routine? Do the routines seem intact and on time, or are some people running late? Who is behind schedule and why? Report (the exchange of on-coming and off-going nurses' information about patients) will commence in five minutes (at 7:00 a.m.) in the conference room. You prepare yourself by reviewing yesterday's assignment sheet, your diary of the tour of duty. After report, you will begin your routines and patient care assignment.

What is a professional nurse's role and its corresponding respon-sibilities? Nursing encompasses planning, implementing, and eval-uating a patient's nursing care needs through assessment of his or her physical, psychological, mental, and emotional status. The expertise with which a nurse meets a patient's needs greatly influences that patient's physical well-being. Preventive mainte-nance, recovery from illness, and decrease in severity of illness are directly affected by the nurse's ability to meet specific patient needs. The nurse must possess the ability to determine the learn-er's readiness to learn, in combination with each individual's comprehension level. The nurse's responsibility is to help each patient learn, retain, and apply the information to his personal activities of daily living.

What does the nurse's daily routine involve? As you might expect, direct patient care is the substance of professional nursing. However, nurses are also involved in teaching patients and their relatives all aspects of health care, or instructing other health care personnel in new procedures or hospital policies. These tasks could include giving or assisting with a.m. (morning) care, which encompasses all aspects of personal hygiene, including bed baths and changing beds. Another possibility is preparing a patient, the bedside unit, and the room for surgery. Checking or starting I.V.'s (intravenous fluids), administering medications, helping patients walk or eat, teaching patients "how to's," charting, consulting with other nurses, discussing patient conditions with other con-cerned professionals, making rounds with physicians, rendering emergency care, intercepting visitors, enforcing hospital rules, and changing surgical dressings are just a few of the routines on most hospital units.

Utilizing the information you have gained thus far, see if you can identify the nurse or the impostor in these three situations.

Details of the Situation: The situation occurs in the front lobby of a nursing home at 3:35 p.m.

A Description of the Mystery Person: The person is a middle-aged male, dressed in a suit and tie. He is immaculately groomed and very businesslike.

Details of the Incident: An elderly man with a walker loses his balance and begins to fall.

Response of the Mystery Person: He responds quickly, preventing the man from falling and supporting him until he regains his balance. The mystery man then summons an office employee to page a floor nurse and bring a wheelchair. Until the nurse arrives, he stays with the resident and instructs him in proper use of the walker, meanwhile doing a quick range-of-motion and eye-pupil check. When the nurse arrives, the mystery man explains the incident, comments on his findings and teachings, and offers a few suggestions.

Is the mystery man most likely a nurse? _X_ Yes _____No

What gave it away? His basic attentiveness to another's needs is innate to the professional nurse. He displayed a high level of alertness to prevent the patient from falling. Teaching and assessment are the trademarks of a successful professional nurse.

Details of the Situation: This event occurs in a quiet, dimly lit private home at 3:00 a.m.

Description of the Mystery Person: The person is a young female, dressed in a robe.

Details of the Incident: Someone falls out of bed and suffers a compound fracture (bone protruding through the skin) of the right leg. The injury has caused severe bleeding.

Response of the Mystery Person: She kneels on the floor next to the injured person. Speaking softly and slowly, she does a complete cardiovascular assessment, checking for signs of shock, while applying pressure to the leg to prevent further blood loss. Without leaving the patient unattended, she covers him and places a pillow under his head. Next, with one eye still on him, she calls an emergency unit. Constantly monitoring his status, she records concise notes on the event and the results.

Is the mystery woman most likely a nurse? _X_ Yes _____No

Her people and technical skills were applied with professional expertise.

Details of the Situation: It is 10:00 a.m., and the incident takes place at a patient's bedside in a hospital.

Description of the Mystery Person: She is a 38-year-old female, wearing a blue dress and white laboratory coat.

Details of the Incident: During a routine venipuncture (withdrawing blood from a vein), the vein ruptures, causing a huge hematoma (bruise).

Response of the Mystery Person: She stops the procedure and explains to the patient what has just happened. She then summons assistance. A second mystery person enters the room, introduces himself, checks the hematoma, applies cool compresses, and tells the patient he will contact the physician.

Is the first mystery person a nurse? _X_ Yes _____No

No, the patient contact was restricted to *one* procedure, obtaining the venipuncture. She was in all probability a laboratory technician.

Is the second mystery person a nurse? _X_ Yes _____No

His direct approach and complete comprehension of the situation leads you to believe he is a professional nurse.

Were any of the four mystery people difficult to identify as nurses or impostors? Some were intended to be a little difficult to demonstrate the versatility of the nurse and erase any conventional stereotypes. Remember, even though clothing and location are indications of whether the mystery person is a nurse or not, the only authentic identification is derived from the individual's personality and activity. By this time, you should recognize the world of nursing as a world of people interested in and ready to help their fellow human beings.

Nursing, A Profession in Transition

Nurses have witnessed, investigated, and encouraged some of the revolutionary changes that have dominated the nursing profession over the last decade. Some changes, such as relaxation of the dress code, have been self-serving and had little effect on other facets of the profession. Other changes, created by outside sources or by nurses themselves, have caused drastic changes in the way nurses think and function.

- The structure of the professional nurse classification is being rebuilt. The nursing profession, and the health care industry in general, have become more business-oriented, concerned with cost-effective, comprehensive patient care. In many hospitals, primary nursing care (one nurse performs all patient care functions for a particular patient, from admission to discharge, on a given shift) has supplanted team nursing (team nurses divide tasks according to classification; one licensed practical nurse (LPN) may pass medications to every patient of the unit).

• Insurance companies and other third-party reimbursement agencies have had a major impact on hospitals' financial controls. One example is DRG's (Diagnosis Related Groups), whereby a health insurance company specifies the maximum amount of money it will pay for a specific illness. Ten years ago, someone having minor surgery, such as a D&C (dilatation and curettage), was admitted and prepped for surgery on day one. On day two, she had the surgery. On day three she was discharged if she was well enough; if not, she stayed an extra day, and her insurance covered the cost. There was no ceiling limit as there is with DRG's. Today, the vast majority of routine D&C's are performed on an outpatient basis. On the morning of the scheduled procedure, the patient arrives at the hospital, is prepped for surgery and sent to the Operating Room. After the surgical procedure is performed, she is sent to the Recovery Room. When she is fully reactive from the anesthetic and her vital signs are stable, usually within a few hours, she is given specific instructions to follow at home. She is then discharged from the Outpatient Surgical Unit. Ten years ago, patients having major surgery were sometimes not allowed to walk for several days. Now, except in rare instances, they are at least sitting on the edge of the bed and dangling their feet within hours after they return to their room from surgery.

Let us analyze the effect that this single control mechanism, the DRG, has on the delivery of health care and the professional nurse's role as a care giver. A shorter hospital stay dictates an intensive, yet concentrated, teaching program, both for the patient and the family. Communication among all hospital staff, especially the patient, nurse, and doctor triage, must be emphasized. Nursing care is compressed, obtaining a higher degree of intensity at an escalated rate. This sophistication of care requires nurses to possess strong observational skills, writing aptitude for documenting patient changes as they happen, and the ability to exercise exact assessment skills to recognize abnormal signs and symptoms before a major complication develops. Shorter hospital stays and advances in accelerated recovery have created a decrease in the total inpatient hospital census, which in turn has reduced hospital profits. Since most hospitals are profit-making institutions, the DRG has compelled hospitals to provide a variety of inpatient and outpatient services in attempts to stay solvent. The traditional inpatient concepts have been replaced by other options, including home health care services, Ambulatory Surgery Units, Health Maintenance Organizations, outpatient units, and community self-help programs.

To survive in a competitive world, hospitals must structure their business to make a profit; budgets must be cost-effective from all aspects. Nurses need to be aware of their hospital's budget status and the percentages slated for patient care, employee salaries, and fringe benefits. Nurses *must* do their share to implement cost-effective, high-quality patient care.

Ten years ago, a nurse probably would not have given a second thought to the cost of a packet of soap or opening a crash cart. In some hospitals, opening the crash cart lock and removing selected contents is a minimum $500 charge to the patient. This cost is relayed to the insurance company, which may or may not, depending on its regulations, reimburse the hospital for the total charge. If the insurance does not cover the expense, the hospital must absorb the loss. Your floor's budget could be the target, which may decrease your regular supply allowance. What is the difference in price between a soapsuds and a fleets enema? Check your local drug store and compare the two. Are you surprised at the difference? To be an all-around successful nurse, you must practice cost containment.

• Hospital administrators now use the media to advertise their special services to the public. Local TV commercials are a favorite vehicle. A decade ago, mounit,tients went to their community hospital when ill. Hospitals now use "cost-effective, good patient care" as their central theme. Several hospitals in a given area may collaborate, form a corporation, and decide which hospital is best equipped and trained to specialize in a specific type of medical problem. Maybe one hospital will choose obstetrics; another, open-heart surgery;

or two or more small hospitals will merge. Find out what all this means to you as a nurse. Talk with a few professionals to discover the dynamics of these changes. Which institution offers the best work environment, provides the services you would like access to, and caters to your nursing specialty?

• The following are some significant changes that warrant your attention. A departmentalized medical staff (department of physicians) works as a unit to streamline medical procedures. Translated, nurses have to meet new procedural requirements as they arise. Today, the majority of physicians more readily accept a nurse's diagnosis than in the past. Many sophisticated new machines are being introduced, both functional and diagnostic, which the nurse must learn to use.

• The nurse's role is expanding rapidly. Are you prepared to ride the wave? A lack of active nurses, insurance reimbursement requirements, Diagnostic Related Groups, changes from traditional inpatient care to outpatient and home-care alternatives, have all created many more opportunities for professional nurses than were available even a few years ago. However, with the added freedom comes added responsibility. For instance, home health care nurses do not have a physician, or another nurse, on the premises. Consider the legal liability in this environment. Are you a candidate for this level of responsibility?

• Nursing educational requirements and standards are not universal, which can confuse a prospective nurse. Some areas of nursing require a specific degree; others do not. Some hospitals pay nurses with an associate degree less than those holding a bachelor of science degree. Some hospitals require specific advanced training before you can work a specialty unit. Cardiac Care requires advanced classroom theory and clinical practicum before you may work with patients. Legislative changes have been proposed to require a professional registered nurse to have a BS degree. Associate degree and diploma RN's would be reclassified to another title of nurse. Continuing education to maintain licensure is another expectation, but not yet required in all states. If a certain degree or specialty training in a particular field of nursing is a major concern to you, contact your state's Nursing Department of Licensing and Regulations. Request an update on the legislation for bachelor of science in nursing (BSN) licensure and mandatory continuing education. Then check with employment prospects in your area to determine the entry level of education each facility requires and how you would obtain advanced specialty training.

* Staffing by acuity is a method of calculating the number of patients each nurse can care for during her shift, depending on the patients' condition. This puts the nurse at the bedside with the patient, eliminates fragmented care, and is cost-effective.

* A new streamlined method of charting has evolved over the last few years, Problem Oriented Recording (POR). Most health organizations have adapted POR or a modification. The method eliminates unnecessary words, promotes charting consistency, saves time, is cost-effective, and decreases paperwork for the nurse.

* Computers are coming of age and becoming another piece of equipment for the nurse to master.

As you can see, nursing has made many changes, adaptations, and advances over the last decade. The profession has gone from white-uniformed female team nursing with limited responsibility, to a relaxed dress code and an infinite number of functional changes, promoting professional expertise in nursing. The nurse, as a result, has accepted more responsibilities; that in turn has influenced the yet unresolved, complex educational requirements for nurses, as well as other professional gray areas. However, the profession has risen to new heights in a relatively short time. With growth and expansion, some growing pains are to be expected.

Opportunities Available to Nurses

The initial health and educational requirements of the nursing profession are universally rigid and inflexible. However, after you have met the health standards, graduated from nursing school, and passed your state boards, you choose your own direction and set your own limits. Your personality and personal resources will dictate your status as a nurse.

The divisions and subdivisions in the field of nursing are awesome in number. It is a matter of choosing the area that best suits your needs and setting attainable, progressive career goals.

Do you prefer direct patient care or administration? What level of management appeals to you, and in which patient-care areas? You can work for an institution, agency, or organization. Self-employment and independent contractual assignments are two other options. Where should you commence? All nursing begins with direct patient care. After studying the following list of a general hospital's inpatient care units, select two or three units that may interest you.

- The Intensive Care Unit deals with the critically ill patient.
- The Cardiac or Coronary Care Unit cares for unstable patients with cardiovascular ailments.
- The Emergency Room is equipped to handle life-or-death situations.
- Obstetrics is the area for a woman about to deliver.
- The Newborn Nursery is where the newborn infant is cared for before going home.
- Postpartum is a unit for new mothers after delivery.
- Gynecology is the unit for women with female problems.
- Orthopedics cares for patients with problems involving the musculoskeletal system.
- Most Psychiatric Units admit emotionally or mentally disturbed persons.
- The Pediatrics Unit is set up for the complete care of ill children.
- A general Medical Unit accommodates anyone requiring medical (noninvasive) treatment for a physical illness.
- The general Surgical Unit provides services for any person in need of surgery (an invasive procedure) to correct a specific ailment.

Does management sound appealing to you? How steep a challenge are you seeking? After you have grasped the fundamental management structure, construct your own game plan.

Commencing with the entry level of management, your climb to the top of the ladder in a basic acute-care hospital management structure would probably resemble this.

- A shift charge nurse is responsible for all nursing functions during that shift. The charge nurse reports to the assistant head nurse or the shift nursing supervisor.

- An assistant head nurse is next in the hierarchy, usually sharing 24-hour unit responsibility with the head nurse. The assistant head nurse reports to the head nurse.
- A head nurse is ultimately responsible for the unit 24 hours a day. The head nurse may report to the shift nursing supervisor or assistant director of nursing.
- The shift nursing supervisor oversees the entire hospital during a specified shift. The shift nursing supervisor reports to the assistant director of nurses.
- The assistant director of nursing services shares responsibility for all nursing personnel, on all units at all times, with the director of nursing. The division of responsibilities depends on the decisions of the director of nursing services.
- The director of nursing services is responsible for the entire nursing department and all of its functions. The director of nursing services report to the hospital administrator.

Where would you like to work? Do any of the following interest you? A hospital, as we have discussed. A long-term-care facility, usually caring for the elderly, or rehabilitative in nature. A clinic for treatment of specific diseases. Your own office, or work for a company based in an office. Other considerations are school, occupational, or industrial nurse.

What percentage of the total responsibility are you willing to shoulder?

- You are not certain; maybe 10 percent.
- You will be fair: You will split it 50-50.
- You know what you are doing: You will accept 75 percent.
- As an independent nurse, you will assume 100 percent.

After establishing the percentage of responsibility you will accept, decide how many hours you are willing to devote to your career.

- You have many nonnursing obligations. You will work less than a 40-hour week.
- You are intelligent and a quick learner. You can achieve your goal in a 40-hour workweek.
- You know your goals and will invest the hours necessary to succeed. You are available for over 40 hours.

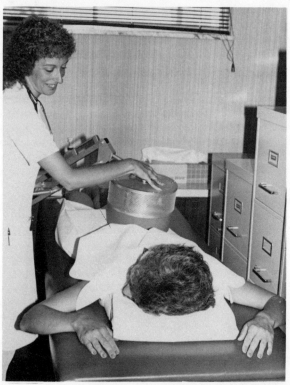

COURTESY KENLOCK CLINIC

In a small rural hospital or a doctor's office the RN performs a variety of nursing functions.

How many hours are you willing to invest in continuing education?

- You do not plan on specializing or going into management. You will take the required, employer-provided inservices to stay current as a professional nurse.
- You have chosen your specialty from the list at the beginning of this section and will pass the required course of study to work the unit.
- You have a perpetual career goals list, involving a patient care specialty or nursing management. You plan to go beyond the

required minimum continuing education to achieve your career aspirations.

What kind of earning potential do you hope to achieve?

- Is $15,000 to $20,000 adequate initially?
- Five years from now will $20,000 to $30,000 meet your changing expectations?
- In ten years will you gross $30,000 plus?

You could conceivably earn $30,000 in five years, but you must cultivate the nursing expertise that warrants your salary demands. Consider these categories.

- What areas of patient care are most appealing to you?
- Is your preference for direct patient care or management?
- Decide where you might enjoy working—perhaps a hospital or a clinic.
- Tabulate the percentage of the total responsibility you are willing to assume, the number of hours you are willing to devote on-the-job, and finally, the resources you are willing to invest in continuing education. Are these three responses compatible with your previous answers? If yes, you have just stated your initial nursing career objectives.

Nurses Come from Many Walks of Life

Just as your opportunities are limited only by your personal fortitude, nurses can and do come from all walks of life. Some start at the bottom and work hard for everything they achieve. Others begin a few rungs closer to the top. See for yourself how three nurses from different environments achieved their individual family and career goals.

Nurse 1 is Carlene Smith, RN, Assistant Director of Nurses and Inservice Director. Carlene lives in a small town in a rural setting. She graduated in 1976 from a diploma (three-year) nursing program. She was employed when she took her state boards. Arranging time off for the exams was not a problem, but working several days in succession before and immediately after the exams was mentally and physically exhausting.

For twelve years Carlene has been employed in a 42-bed acute-care hospital. Nurses at her hospital still wear white uniforms, but the nurse's cap is optional. From 1973 to 1984, Carlene's role was an RN (registered nurse) staff nurse, performing direct patient care and relief charge nurse duties. Charge duties at this small hospital include every unit: Obstetrics, Pediatrics, Cardiac Care, and Emergency Room on weekends. Carlene had declined promotions in the past, but in 1984 she accepted appointment to assistant director of nursing and inservice director. She is also pursuing her BSN degree.

Nurse 2 is Christine Bekish, an RN and a nursing home administrator. In contrast to Carlene's rural setting, Chris lives in Woodhaven, a small town not far from metropolitan Detroit. In 1966 Chris graduated with a three-year diploma. She was employed at the time of her state boards and had no problem getting time off for the exams.

After spending her initiation time in an acute-care hospital, Chris resigned and went to work for Beverly Manor Nursing Homes. Employed first as inservice director, she was then promoted to director of nursing. After additional educational preparation and passing the Nursing Home Administrator's State Board exam, she received her administrator's license. For six years Chris has been a nursing home administrator, responsible for all functions and all departments of a 144-bed nursing home on a 24-hour basis. Chris must take 18 hours of continuing education annually to maintain her status as a nursing home administrator.

Nurse 3 is Jackie Heron, RN, Executive Director, consultant, and published author. Jackie has lived in a rural setting and been employed in a large city most of her life. She graduated from an associate degree RN program. She, too, was employed at the time of state boards and had no difficulty getting time off to take the exams.

After spending two years in a Lansing hospital (over 300 beds), Jackie left for the fast track. She accepted employment at a university medical center and simultaneously enrolled in classes at an affiliated university. After indoctrination at a hospital of over 1,000 beds and studying in two specialties, she returned to Lansing. Her next appointment was director of nursing at a home health agency. Six months later she was appointed branch director of two offices. One year later Jackie became director of nursing of a rural acute-care hospital, followed by director of nursing of a 144-bed nursing home. Jackie has taken her Nursing Home Administrator's boards and is a senior in the Health Care Administration bachelor's degree program.

Just for fun, if you have put the pieces together, you have

deduced that Carlene was a staff RN and relief charge nurse for Jackie while she was director of nursing services at a rural hospital. Chris was Jackie's immediate supervisor while Jackie was director of nursing of the nursing home. Three nurses with very different backgrounds who still were very successful. Your background may influence your decisions, but it does not have to be the controlling factor.

Reader's Review

Reflect for a moment on what you have read. Every situation revolves around human beings and their emotional, intellectual, and psychosocial well-being. Nurses play a major role in directing the way those they encounter recover from surgery, react to traumatic experiences, or respond to a procedure.

As you read this book, think seriously about your future. What type of person are you? What do you want out of life, and how hard are you willing to work for it? What are your motives for becoming a nurse? Which are the most important to you, and which the least important? Only you know whether respect and recognition, a sense of achievement, a desire to help someone in need, or financial rewards is your deepest desire. Be truthful with yourself and you will make the right decision.

True or False

A. Nursing is a people-oriented profession.
B. Nurse are being threatened by the robotics invasion.
C. Nurses are often scheduled to work shifts other than 9:00 a.m. to 5:00 p.m.
D. Ability to read and follow directions carefully is a definite asset.
E. High moral and ethical standards are of little or no value in the world of nursing.

(B and E are false; A,C, and D are true.)

Satisfaction envelops you if you love nursing. Which of these activities give you positive strokes?

• Having a quiet visit with a critically ill, homebound person.

- Helping another person walk down the steps.
- Learning how to take blood pressure.
- Teaching someone to perform cardiopulmonary resuscitation.
- Consulting with a physician to learn more about a specific disease.
- Talking and listening as a depressed friend describes a crisis.
- Consoling a grief-stricken family when their loved one has expired.

Quite possibly, all of them? Congratulations! Each one directly or indirectly assists a patient. If there are some you would actively avoid, make a mental note of caution; you may wish to steer clear of that type of patient care. If death and dying depress you, do not pursue a position with Hospice, which deals exclusively with persons who are dying.

Nursing is a profession in transition. Which of the following has remained unchanged?

A. The professional nurses' dress code.
B. The basic structure of the health-care delivery system.
C. A professional nurse's innate personality traits.

(C is correct.)

Take a few moments to read and absorb the following illustration. Its specific purpose is to elicit your innermost thoughts and feelings.

It is the scene of an accident. The front-seat passenger's leg is crushed and bleeding; the victim looks dead. The driver was thrown through the windshield. Fragments of glass penetrated his head and show through his hair. His eyes glare up at you as you look down at him. His trunk is stiff, but his arms and legs lie limp.

What are your first, second, and third thoughts or emotional-logical reactions?

- This is a grisly mess, and you feel weak inside. It is best for everyone if you depart.
- Look at the traffic pileup! You will be late for the game.
- You should get out and help, but you do not have a change of clothes nor a way to clean up after.

- Why stick around? You would not know what to do. You would only be in the way.
- You ask if anyone has called an ambulance and the police.
- Should you park your car and offer emergency first aid until the paramedics arrive?

What were your perceptions through your senses?

- What did you see? Two severely injured people lying helpless on the cold, hard pavement.
- What did you hear from the victims? Dead silence.
- What did you touch? Two unconscious human beings whose skin was clammy and blue, with lots of blood.
- What did you smell? Smoldering car engines and burned rubber.
- What did you feel? Emotions ranging from fear, tension, empathy, and sympathy, to sadness.

What were your physiological reactions?

- Nausea and marked weakness offset by a sudden surge of energy. Your accelerated thought process kicked in as adrenaline rose to aid you in your rescue efforts.
- Direct bodily changes included an increased heart rate and pulse, labored breathing, and hyperventilation. These cardiovascular and pulmonary changes caused chest palpitations.
- Muscle fatigue overwhelmed you as you strained to execute life-sustaining cardiac massage.

What were your mental-logical reactions as you watched the emergency squad begin to aid the accident victims?

- Will either man live? What will be the quality of his life if he is revived? What will his recovery be like? Will there be irreversible neurological damage to the head injury patient?
- How will this accident and its aftermath affect family members? What long-term results are reasonably predictable?
- What about yourself? How will this accident scene change your driving habits? What if you had been in that car at that precise moment?
- How did your rescue efforts affect you as a nurse? Were they adequate or weak?

- Digging deeper, what caused the accident? Were drugs or alcohol responsible? Could it have been avoided?

What were your emotional reactions?

- Did you feel empathy and sadness for the victims? Did you feel compassion for the family and friends of the injured men?
- Did you fear that the same fate could befall you, or a loved one?

What were your psychological reactions? What coping mechanisms did you employ?

- "It won't happen to me" is a popular one.
- Or the classic denial, or complete suppression of the accident.

If this illustration leaves you with a slight gastrointestinal disturbance, the Emergency Room probably will not be your favorite unit.

There are no right or wrong answers to any of these questions, only your subjective responses. The bottom line of this chapter is that the desire for human involvement is the overriding characteristic of the nurse.

Chapter II

The Dynamics of a Successful Nurse

Successful nurses are male or female, eighteen to sixty-five, of any religion, race, color, or creed. They come from all walks of life and live anywhere, worldwide. Successful professional nurses are a highly diversified group of people possessing a wide variety of personality traits. Successful nurses recognize and capitalize on their own particular skills and attributes.

Before you can decide whether you would be a successful nurse, you must compare successful nurses' assets and idiosyncrasies with your own. Knowing your own personality will help you determine your potential level of success as a professional nurse. In this chapter, use the case histories, situational questions, and supplemental self-helps to draw a blueprint of your personality and that of a successful nurse. Compare your likes and dislikes, philosophies, and dominating features to those of a successful nurse. After gaining this perspective, you should discover your starting point in the world of nursing.

The Six Key Ingredients of Successful Nursing

Common Sense + Logic + Professional Technical Skills + Formal Nursing Education + Health Requirements + People Skills = The Successful Nurse.

According to the dictionary, common sense is the reliable ability of the average person to make an intelligent decision without sophisticated knowledge on a given subject. Do you have good common sense?

It is 5:00 a.m. and you cannot find the peanut butter for the diabetics' supplemental feeding. What should you do?

A. Call the director of nurses and ask for help.
B. Omit the 6:00 a.m. feeding; the patient is asleep anyway.

    C. Find a suitable supplemental replacement; for instance, cheese and crackers.

C is your best response. Why? Because 5:00 a.m. is not a good time to call the director with a question you can answer yourself. Chances are excellent that he or she has put in at least eight hours and will return to duty in a few hours. B is a dangerous answer. Omitting a supplemental feeding can cause serious consequences for a diabetic, not to mention your professionalism. You would be legally liable for willful and deliberate patient neglect. Your credibility as a conscientious nurse would be in jeopardy. Yes, the patient is asleep; however, many diabetics awake hungry when their supplement is due.

You thought that was simple? It was, if you think like most professional nurses.

Merriam-Webster defines logic as "the formal principles of reasoning" that allow you to reach a conclusion. If your reasoning process is logical, you will follow a sequence of steps that are sensible and easily duplicated by another. Even though other people may not arrive at the same conclusion, they can readily follow and understand your reasoning. Logic is often directly related to problem-solving.

You have a doctor's order to give a medication that can be administered by mouth or by injection. The patient in question has suffered gastrointestinal upset, nausea and vomiting, and has been unable to keep any food down for the last four hours. What actions would you take?

    A. Give the medicine by mouth because the patient hates shots and you detest giving them.

    B. Give the medicine by mouth and pray it stays down.

    C. Give the patient an intramuscular injection.

In the absence of nausea and vomiting, the medicine by mouth would have been a logical response. Since the patient has suffered from uncontrolled vomiting for four hours, logic suggests that he probably would not be able to keep the medicine down either. To prevent his having further abdominal irritation and possibly severe pain, you opt to give him an injection.

People skills are of paramount importance in nursing. The world of nursing involves other people on every surface. Review these hypothetical situations and decide in which of them you acted on impulse, in which you reacted intelligently, and in which you interacted with others. The situations have some gray areas but may help you to develop self-awareness.

A. A patient unfairly and angrily lashes out at you. Caught off guard, you vehemently defend yourself vocally.
B. During the patient-care conference, you contribute valuable ideas to the care plan and exchange ideas with others.
C. You find a patient unresponsive and not breathing. Immediately you initiate cardiopulmonary resuscitation.

Situation A is an impulsive, emotional response.
Situation B is an interaction with other professionals.
Situation C is an intelligent reaction to a situation.

If you disagree with the analysis, that is fine, provided you analyze your behavior. Attempt to determine when you are acting on impulse, reacting intelligently, or interacting with others.

Professional technical skills are specific, scientifically based skills that you must master fully before you are qualified to perform the functions of a professional nurse. Professional technical skills range from the fundamental nursing techniques of bed-making and transferring a patient from wheelchair to bed, all the way to complex procedures such as cardiovascular assessment and controlling sophisticated equipment such as monitors and respirators. Do you have the perseverance to practice the basic skills one by one until you have mastered each? Do you possess the insight to recognize when you need help? Do you have the self-confidence to seek guidance from the appropriate resource person when necessary?

Basic Educational Requirements for Professional Nurses

Formal nursing education constitutes a prescribed curriculum of theory and clinical nursing classes. Minimum educational requirements are one full year of training for licensed practical nurses; two years (associate degree) for registered nurses; and four years to earn a bachelor of science in nursing degree. Although not mandatory, the BSN is a distinct advantage in most cases. After graduation, all registered nurses must take and pass three-day state board examinations before being licensed to practice nursing. Intensive preparation is often necessary to meet state licensure requirements. LPNs take a one-day state examination.

Do you possess the drive, desire, and intelligence to meet the educational demands of the nursing profession? Calculate the effort you intend to invest in your career before you decide whether you want the challenge. The rewards you reap in nursing are usually in direct proportion to the effort you put forth.

Basic Health Requirements for the Professional Nurse

Holistic health is of prime importance. You must be in touch with your intimate state of being and practice good health habits to keep your mental, psychological, emotional, and physical properties intact. A malfunction or illness in one of the four interrelated aspects can be reflected in your performance. A severe mental, emotional, or psychological ailment would bar you from entering the nursing profession. Physical handicaps, depending on the degree of incapacitation, can limit or have minimal effect on your nursing career. The hearing-impaired cannot work a specialty unit that requires acute auditory senses to hear the sophisticated machines. One confined to a wheelchair would be physically unable to perform direct patient-care duties. However, if you have a disorder that can be controlled and does not adversely affect your daily activities you could still be an excellent nurse. An actual advantage for nurses with diabetes or other health disorders is their ability to relate to patients with the same affliction. Patients can identify with, and often communicate with, a nurse who shares their illness.

Personal Characteristics of a Successful Nurse

Your personal characteristics are the capabilities, habits, mannerisms, attributes, and qualities that make you uniquely you.

- Successful nurses are selfless by nature and care about the welfare of others. They make personal effort and sometimes personal sacrifice to help other human beings to meet their needs, whether complex or simple.
- The successful nurse is adaptable, rearranging his or her lifestyle to accommodate both professional and social aspirations.
- Empathy and compassion for others are indispensable attributes.
- Sensitivity and tact in handling stressful situations can avert a potential disaster.
- Patience is conducive to a therapeutic atmosphere.

- An objective, nonjudgmental attitude to others can help you achieve mutual goals with minimum effort and maximum efficiency.
- The ability to compromise can be the difference between a pleasant or an unsatisfactory work environment. If, on the contrary, you compromise your professional, ethical, or moral standards, the compromise could have devastating results.
- Being a self-starter keeps your supervisor and your patients happy. Taking the initiative potentiates a positive interaction between you and significant others.
- Flexibility in all facets of your tour of duty will help you accomplish routine tasks and handle unexpected emergencies.
- Quick learning, retention, and ability to apply what you have learned are not requirements but are a definite asset. An enormous amount of information is necessary in nursing; you must know it, learn it, or know exactly where to find it in a hurry.
- Public relations skills can help you solidify your position as a respected nurse and community member.
- Accuracy, completeness, and attention to detail greatly enhance your efficiency in all areas of nursing.
- Personal integrity and fortitude are essential.
- Perseverance and persistence to overcome obstacles (real or imagined) and meet deadlines cement the personality structure of the successful nurse.
- Versatility and stability enable you to handle two or more activities simultaneously. These two assets are invaluable in a high-stress, fast-paced unit such as Intensive Care.
- Honest, accurate presentation of information is mandatory. Exaggerations, underestimations, or word games can result in lawsuits. The death of a patient can be the end product of misinformation.
- Self-confidence is contagious. If you believe in yourself, others will believe in you and you will perform on an elevated level.

Ask yourself some pertinent questions.

- Are you always approachable, or do people have to decide whether you are in a good mood? You will be omitted from many concerns that directly affect you if others have to guess whether it is safe to talk to you. Management positions would become elusive. Establishing and maintaining rapport with people would

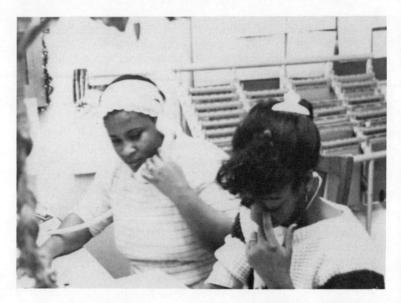

COURTESY BEVERLY MANOR

A concerned nurse contacts a patient's physician while a coworker catches up on her charting.

be next to impossible. Your credibility could suffer because of your lack of involvement. Approachability does not mean dropping what you are doing the instant you are asked. It simply means being responsive, receptive, and open to the concerns of others, being able to say pleasantly, "I am busy at the moment; what would be a convenient time for me to get back to you?"

• Do you have a soft-spoken, passive disposition, or are you energetic and assertive? Either disposition can make a successful nurse, providing you pursue a field of nursing compatible with your personality. An assertive, energetic person would probably love the bustle of the large research hospital. The passive person is more likely to succeed in patient and staff teaching, or Rehabilitative Nursing.

- Are you comfortable with abstract ideas and a free-flowing atmosphere, or are you in a fog unless you are in a highly structured setting with concrete facts to build on? Both personality types could be successful in the appropriate setting. The highly structured personality would most likely do well in a specialty unit, and the free-flowing might choose Psychiatric Nursing.

- Are you a realist or an idealist? Both are well suited for nursing, as long as they recognize their characteristics and accept their limitations. Extreme idealism leads to fantasy-type expectations. Excessive realism can take the last gleam of hope from a critically ill patient. When the will to live is broken, death is usually imminent in the critical patient. On the other hand, it is a long fall from that castle in the sky. In other words, neither extreme is permissible.

- Are you a pessimist or an optimist? A pessimist can create, be responsible for, contribute to, and thus be confronted with more problems than the reasonably optimistic person will ever encounter. If you look for a dark side, you can usually find it; chase it often, and people will show you only that side. Pessimism is better left to another profession, maybe boxing.

- Are you impractical or practical? Impractical people have more difficulty adjusting to nursing than the practical, because of the scientific structure of nursing.

- Do you utilize a perfected thought process, or are you a random thinker extracting answers from existing evidence? Random thinkers will not find it easy to follow the scientific process used to answer questions. Consequently, they may face some hurdles.

- Are you quick-tempered? Occasionally even the seasoned veteran makes mistakes and is overwhelmed with confusion for a brief moment. If you have a short fuse, your co-workers will not give you the support you need to lift you out of the chaos. Instead, they will avoid the explosion, you, like the plague.

- Are you overly sensitive? If so, your feelings may be hurt unnecessarily. When people are displaced, such as in the hospital, their own insecurities and fears have to be ventilated. At times the nurse is the target. A patient may be worried about his job, but if it takes you eight minutes instead of three to get him a pain killer, you are blamed for his backache.

- If others perceive you as abrasive and critical, you will not fare well in this profession. You must be people-oriented. Abrasive people create more conflicts and confrontations than management will tolerate. If you have a tendency to be critical, be certain that your criticism is accurate and justified. Check your own record before making statements: When did you last commit the same error you are ridiculing, or worse yet, a more serious one?

• Are you defensive and quick with excuses if you commit an error? Save it for the incident report. All mistakes are documented for review by an appointed board. If you have a legitimate reason for the mistake, you can tell the world, but chances are that it will fall on deaf ears. We all make mistakes; we learn from them and grow professionally. Making an issue of an error is self-defeating. Are you overly defensive and protective of your actions if you are ridiculed by a co-worker? Examine why this upsets you. Are you insecure, or ashamed to admit the truth? Or are you afraid of the results of your mistake, or possibly resentful or jealous of your critic's expertise or status?

• Are you easily deceived? Be prepared to be taken advantage of until you learn to distinguish friend from foe and fact from fiction. It will not hinder your nursing in the technical aspect, but it could stifle advancement within the system.

• Can you build your own network of professionals who complement one another and activate a support system that nurtures professional maturation and advancement? Although not a necessity, this is an ability that will speed your progress up the ladder of success.

• Are you shy? Consistently or only in isolated incidents? If consistently, constant interaction with people may not be ideal for you. Are incidents of shyness likely to affect you at work, and to what extent will they influence or interfere with your nursing duties? Do large crowds petrify you? That should have no effect on your ability to function as a nurse unless you were to volunteer for the rescue mission of a national disaster.

• After you have made a decision, are you confident that you have used sound judgment? Or can a convincing argument easily change your mind, even without substantiating evidence? Every day you make hundreds of decisions in nursing, some life-dependent and some incidental. If every decision you make haunts you, you will have a tremendous mental block in coping with your patient care assignment.

• Do you support, accept, or bristle at change? Nursing is fast-paced. Technical advances are an integral part of the profession and occur frequently, occasionally without warning.

- Are you a leader, an active contributor, a rebel, a fence sitter, or a follower? The leader leads himself to a chosen destination. All other factors being equal, the contributor can excel or advance rapidly if he or she proceeds methodically. The fence sitter must be cautious not to sit too long, lest he fall in the quicksand instead of jumping to safety. The follower adapts to a level of personal and professional expertise that will satisfy everyone. Even the rebel can fit the professional mold, with a few modifications. When the cause that a rebel supports and fights for meets the needs of the majority of the people, the characteristic becomes constructive. Each trait, when properly applied, can bring personal and professional success.

- Are you a fast or slow thinker? Do you work quickly and precisely, or slowly and methodically? Both have their virtues, and each can be a star on the right stage. A fast mover can be a detriment to the physical, social, emotional, mental, and psychological well-being of a patient in a rehabilitative unit. There, people need to progress at their own pace, without pressure to perform beyond their readiness level. A slow thinker and mover could be a disaster in Cardiac Care. A life-saving maneuver delayed by seconds can cause irreversible damage.

  To know thyself is to avert misery. A case in point: An excellent registered nurse graduated from a four-year nursing program with honors. After spending three months in a fast-paced Cardiac Care Unit, she was a basket case and felt a failure. After much introspection, she resigned and went into Public Health Nursing, at which she is uncannily adept and very successful.

- Can you effectively execute more than one task at a time amid interference and confusion? Could you stop while passing medications, handle an acute emergency (an incoherent patient pulled his chest tube out), then return to the medications without losing control of the situation? Could you leave your routine duties to help another nurse in a bad predicament, and when peace was restored return to your own work?

- Are you quiet and calm, or easily excited? If you can juggle more than one task at a time, cope with serious interruptions, and transfer easily from your duties to another, a specialty unit could interest you. If you prefer a calmer atmosphere, you could be a definite asset to Self-Care, Psychiatric Nursing, Rehabilitation, Geriatrics, inservice director, or other nursing options.

- Are you a good team member, or more effective as a loner? Either can be successful in nursing, depending on the job setting. A loner could profit from a doctor's office setting, whereas a team member does well in a hospital.

• If routine bores you, you will want to avoid or compensate for it as much as possible. It is difficult to avoid completely.

• Are you willing to study nursing on your own time, occasionally at your own expense? In some states, legislation has already been passed requiring a specific amount of continuing education annually for renewal of nursing licenses. Even if such legislation does not materialize in your state, without supplemental education you may not be able to maintain your present status.

• Is financial reward more valuable to you than emotional and personal satisfaction? If money is your major objective, you may choose to investigate other options. Nurses' salaries are competitive with most other fields, education and qualifications being equal; but you have missed the real depth of nursing. Nursing is multidimensional: people working for and with people, and the rewards are reciprocal.

• Are you easily depressed when around ill people? Do certain afflictions appall or disgust you (alcoholism, drug abuse, disfigurement)? You may want to investigate more thoroughly what it is about ill people that depresses you. If you have a strong transference, you can capitalize on that and use it to help another. If the depression overwhelms you or leaves you unpredictably down, maybe nursing is not for you. Nurses are involved in preventive maintenance, but people still contract diseases; some are born with congenital anomalies. Even if you plan to set up your own consulting business, the central theme of your nurses' training is still *care of the ill*, and you must complete your training before you can be licensed.

• Attitude is one of those intangibles that most people do not define, but everyone knows what it is. Attitude is a culmination of your personal self. You have taken a lifetime to learn and acquire your attitude. A good attitude is expected in nursing and often goes unrewarded; but a bad attitude is frequently the cause of problems and is quickly reprimanded. The importance of a good attitude is often underrated. Nurses with excellent technical, clinical practicum and educational qualifications have been released because of serious conflicts when the underlying cause was really a bad attitude. Nothing compensates for a bad attitude. A negative, nothing-ever-goes-right, I-hate-to-work-here, know-it-all attitude is usually surrounded by needless problems, providing the director with ammunition to take disciplinary action against the guilty person. Most directors of nursing are adept at spotting a bad attitude a mile away. During an interview, a nurse with a good attitude and lesser professional expertise (providing it is not substandard) will most likely be hired. The technically proficient nurse with an unyielding attitude will be rejected. Skills and attitude are not synonymous, but a good attitude can go far in gaining you the guidance and support you need to nurture your technical skills. On the contrary, a bad attitude can be a direct ticket to the unemployment office.

- Technical skills are acquired through extensive and intensive training and practice. Skills can be taught to someone willing to learn.
- Your philosophy, religious convictions, moral and ethical values, standards of judgment, prejudices (we all have them, even if against violence or abuse), and political affiliations are the covert factors that mold your personal attitude and characteristics. Be consciously aware of the influence each entity exerts on your work. Then gain control of the negative factors by restraining or compensating for them.
- Interpersonal skills are imperative, the trademark of a successful nurse. If you possess the innate ability to read another person's written, unspoken, and oral messages and process that information to help the person accomplish a specific task, you have excellent people skills. If you can understand, interpret, analyze, decipher, anticipate, and assist others to express their feelings constructively and completely, you have multidimensional interpersonal skills.
- Are you able to evaluate and teach patients how to reach their optimum health potential psychologically, physiologically, emotionally, and mentally? This means promoting healthy attitudes while developing coping skills that foster emotional and mental stability.
- Communication is the cohesive element of nursing. If you possess good oral, written, and silent communication skills, you will effectively relate to everyone in a variety of situations. Oral communication consists of the words you speak. Oral communication is the fastest form of communication, but it has its drawbacks. Once spoken, you cannot have those words back. Oral communication is hard-hitting, with fast, direct results. There is great virtue in knowing what to say, when to say it, how to say it, and when to shut up. The spoken word should be exchanged with, not projected at, or spoken down to another. Body language is quiet, yet powerful, communication. Everyone sends messages with their body move-

ments. Some people read and understand them; others do not. Your body is always talking, even as you are reading this book. What are you telling yourself and others? Think about your body language.
• Are you a good listener? Do you hear what people are telling you as they tell it? Do you consciously or unconsciously slant your interpretation to meet your standards? Good listening is quite possibly the least perfected, and most widely neglected, form of communication. Feedback and open-ended questions are two reliable methods of assuring understanding of the sender's statement and its exact intention. Here is an example:

Nurse Receiver:	"You said yesterday was a bad day. Exactly what went wrong?"
Patient Sender:	"I was weak, tired, and hurt all over. To top it off, my dinner was cold, and the baseball game was rained out."
Nurse Receiver:	"Did you tell your nurse or your doctor about your weakness, fatigue, and hurting all over?"
Patient Sender:	"No, everyone was too busy to listen."
Nurse Receiver:	"Are you still feeling weak? Which baseball game was rained out? Are you an avid baseball fan?"

The nurse continues with her questions until she has identified all the issues and isolated the most important factors. An effective listener can coax a patient to reveal critically important secrets.
• Accurate written skills are a must for legal documentation on charts, nursing care plans, and insurance forms.

Step 1: List four or more personality traits you consider to be your assets. Decide how each trait has contributed to your success as a person? For example, common sense and logic let you understand most of the behavioral transactions you are involved in. Flexibility and adaptability allow you to adjust to change. Listening to someone's message at the right moment may garner information that left to simmer may go unsaid. Sensitivity to the needs of others is synonymous with "I feel for you." Patience lets you effectively handle a crisis. Empathy permits others to identify with you and establish rapport.

Step 2: List at least two less-than-perfect traits you possess. Maybe you are a perfectionist, and consequently hypercritical of others. Perhaps retaining learned facts is difficult for you.

Identify specific problems these traits have contributed to or caused. Perfectionism transferred to other people can create many personality conflicts. Difficulty in retaining learned material can interfere with your social life because of the extra study time required to achieve your goal. Now exercise a little introspection: How have you compensated for your shortcomings? You can use three methods to control your perfectionism: You do not judge others by your standards of perfection; you do not expect more from a co-worker than his or her ability allows, unless performance falls below minimum standards; and you recognize that no one is perfect. To help you retain facts, you practice tricks to enhance your memory.

In a job interview, a director of nurses looks for specific personality traits that will complement her institutional needs. Every director looks for desirable traits and recognizes that we all have flaws. If your interviewer asks what your shortcomings are, tell her; *then*, back it up with your compensatory action.

Professional technical skills are the nursing tasks you must perform to deliver patient care. Knowledge of the mechanics and theory of professional technical skills is the core of the nursing profession. Proficient practical, clinical application of the technical skills and supporting theory is a challenge all nurses must meet and conquer. Lacking this, you are not a nurse. How do you know what they are? How can you prepare yourself? Each nursing school teaches the material in its own way. Some people have a natural ability to master the mechanical aspects of bed-making, while others easily comprehend the theory of why square corners are used. Be assured, it is a rare person who cannot master both in the time allotted. Learn the principles of theory and clinical practice as they are taught. That is the best insurance against catastrophe. Why? Simply because nursing begins with basic scientific facts. You build on these facts as you increase your nursing knowledge. Your theory and clinical practicum become progressively more difficult in direct relation to the scientific principles you have learned. First, learn the mechanical function: how to take blood pressure. Second, add the theory: What is blood pressure and what does it tell you about a patient's condition? The third building block distinguishes normal blood pressure from abnormal, and the fourth discusses the treatment of abnormal blood pressure. Take the time to practice every detail over and over again until it becomes an automatic reaction. If you do this, you will not feel like a beginner when you are assigned patients.

General skills are everyday skills; they are not nursing skills per se, but they can make your tour of duty a little easier.

• Ability to anticipate patient needs and forthcoming events is invaluable. It minimizes negative stress and could save a patient's life.

• Observational skills can mean the difference between life and death. To observe does not mean just to look; it means to *see* the most minute changes and know what to do about each. Without this skill, your professional technical skills are limited and your value as a nurse is severely restricted.

• Everyone talks about time management, but no one does it to perfection. Because nursing has so many variables, beginning with the human element, no one can predict when a crisis will arise or when a patient will become acutely ill.

• Negotiating with others to arrive at an agreement acceptable to all concerned parties is a frequent occurrence.

• You should adopt a scientific approach to problem solving, one that can be readily duplicated and understood because of its logical sequence of steps. The following illustration offers a simplistic problem-solving process. To test the method, work through a problem or two yourself.

You are habitually late leaving work, and the oncoming nurse, even though punctual, is consistently tardy beginning her tour of duty.

A *preliminary assessment* indicates a time-management problem during shift change. The patient-care reports always start at their scheduled time of 11:00 p.m. but are rarely finished by 11:30 p.m. The professional standards of both nurses are quite similar. Each is detail-oriented, knowledgeable, conscientious, proficient, and frustrated by a time-management problem.

Your *plan of action* is to adopt a time-management program applicable to both parties. Both nurses begin by reexamining the contents of patient-care reports. They eliminate nonessential details without adversely affecting the quality of the report. Is all the information given during report relevant to the existing circumstances? Yes, it is. Could report be given while making patient rounds? Yes, talking and walking accomplishes two goals simultaneously.

The *expected outcome* is effective and efficient time management, reducing or eliminating negative stress.

An *evaluation* indicates that the problem has improved, but both nurses are still ten minutes late most of the time.

Proposed changes include trying to condense report more by recording routine data on the chart sheets for quick reference and giving oral report on only the abnormalities.

A *time frame* is established, and the nurses check their time-management progress daily until the problem is resolved.

A *final evaluation* shows that within five days both nurses are on schedule, and all duties are performed on a timely basis.

Is this problem-solving process too much to bother with? Not really, because a logical thought process is a dependable method of collecting, compiling, analyzing, resolving, and evaluating all the facts before initiating an effective plan of action. You can modify this format to suit your special needs, and with practice the process becomes automatic.

Every nursing decision you make has hidden implications, and the effects can be widespread. In our example, patients, nurses, physicians, and other related hospital departments could be affected by the time-management problem. The change in documentation, incorporating more written facts and decreasing oral report, could conceivably filter through to the state board of accreditation and other governing agencies. Remember, the state board and significant other governing agencies have access to and do read patients' charts. Make your decisions count in a favorable way.

Adeptness at problem-solving prevents unnecessary hassles and reduces friction considerably, allowing you to proceed with your plan of action as established in prioritizing, organizing, and time management.

- Prioritizing is deciding what should be done first and the order in which remaining tasks are to be completed. It means separating the important from the less important; distinguishing the must-do-immediately (STAT) cardiopulmonary resuscitation from the IV medication that should be run from 8:00 to 8:30 a.m., and from the complete bed bath that must be finished before 3:00 p.m.
- Organizational skills are essential to successful completion of the daily routine during your tour of duty. You schedule tasks according to priorities and your predetermined time frame for commencing and ending the assignment. You monitor and rearrange your schedule according to your work load.

Setting priorities, organizing your day, managing your time, and resolving your problems are interrelated in nursing. It is virtually impossible to succeed at one unless you are proficient at all of them. Priorities are like the gas in your car; without the ignition (organization), you are at a standstill. Time management is your control of the acceleration, and problems are like the brakes being applied in the middle of the fast lane on the expressway.

From the information provided below, decide how you should prioritize, organize, and let time manage your day.

- Your shift is 7:00 a.m. to 3:30 p.m. You are allowed two 15-minute coffee breaks and a 1/2-hour lunch break.
- You must make patient rounds twice, once in the morning, and again in the afternoon. Patient rounds take about 30 minutes each time.
- The IV's in rooms 410 bed 1, 414 bed 2, 418 bed 2, and 422 private room were last checked at 7:00 a.m., and must be checked every 1/2 hour.
- Medications are to be passed at 10:00 a.m. and 2:00 p.m. Each round takes about 1/2 hour.
- Your 1/2-hour lunch break is scheduled for 11:30 a.m. Your patients eat lunch at noon.
- Oncoming nursing report has already been given and can be disregarded. You are still responsible for shift change report between 3:00 and 3:30 p.m.

Here is a sample worksheet you can use as a guide.

- The IV's were last checked at 7:00 a.m.; it is 7:30 a.m. They need to be checked every 1/2 hour, which is now, and it takes 15 minutes.
- At 8:00 a.m. you commence your patient a.m. care. At 8:30 a.m., you check IV's and offer patients assistance as needed.
- From 8:30 to 9:00 a.m. you check IV's and help those in need with their personal care.
- Between 9:00 and 9:30 a.m., you complete your patients' a.m. care.
- From 9:30 to 10:00 a.m. you check the IV's and set up the IV medications as you make rounds.
- From 10:00 to 10:30 a.m., you pass medications.
- From 10:30 to 11:00 a.m., during your IV check, you complete all IV medications started at 10:00 a.m.
- You spend 11:00 to 11:30 a.m. doing your morning charting.

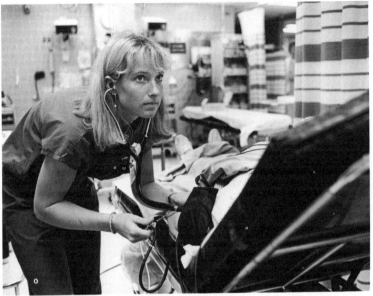

COURTESY WILLIAM BEAUMONT HOSPITAL
A nurse monitors a patient's blood pressure.

- At 11:30 a.m. is your most-welcome lunch break. Another nurse checks your IV's and attends to your patients in your absence. You will reciprocate when that nurse goes to lunch.
- At noon, you return to your unit and commence patient rounds, to observe appetites and note worthwhile facts. During your patient rounds, a patient chokes, resulting in a large emesis in which he soils himself, his bed, and the floor. You stop what you are doing, and from the patient's bedside you call housekeeping to clean the floor. You help your patient start his bath. While he is bathing, you strip his bed and remake it.
- From 12:20 to 1:00 p.m. you resume your patient rounds and check IV's.
- At 12:30 p.m. you check back on your ill patient's progress, which is as expected at this time. Before 12:45 p.m., your

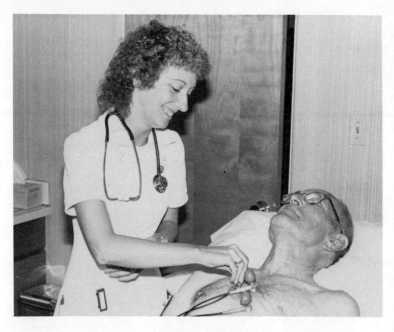

An RN performs an EKG.

COURTESY KENLOCK CLINIC

patient is clean, freshly gowned, resting comfortably in his recliner, and his bed is ready for him.

* Between 1:00 and 1:15 p.m. you begin charting.
* From 1:15 to 2:00 p.m. you combine your p.m. care with checking IV's.
* Between 2:00 and 2:30 p.m., you pass routine medications and check IV's.
* You finish your shift charting between 2:30 and 3:00 p.m.
* From 3:00 to 3:30 p.m., you give your shift report to the oncoming nurse.

Notice the flow if your prioritized organization and scheduling fall into place naturally. Both 15-minute breaks were omitted. What is a logical time for each? You have 15 minutes unaccounted for between each IV check throughout the day.

Mechanical aptitude is an attribute, not a requirement or even an expectation. However, it helps you learn to use, maintain, and understand simple mechanical processes and make minor adjustments to a machine to conserve time and energy and avoid confusion and nerves. An intravenous pump malfunction may be remedied with your fingertip or require master craftsmanship. Lacking mechanical aptitude, you will be forced to consult someone more knowledgeable. Proper use and maintenance of equipment helps prevent malfunctions. At least a basic understanding of the mechanics of a complex unit such as the cardiopulmonary respirator, with its awesome sound system, would be helpful. Some signals indicate that all is well (a beep for each breath). Others produce sounds of happiness, telling you the patient is improving. A ring may indicate that your patient took an unsupported, spontaneous breath. A third alarm warns of impending complications, such as that a patient's heart has arrested. The fourth may inform you that the machine has gone haywire. This sophisticated apparatus can be your best friend, a robot nurse in your absence, if you understand it; it can be an implacable enemy if it controls or intimidates you.

Reader's Review

Let us create an image of a successful nurse by drawing a "word image" of yourself.

Step 1: State all your personal data, including the age you will be when you graduate from nursing school, your sex, your cultural background as it pertains to nursing, and any other facts you feel would be a positive influence.

Step 2: Summarize your personal attributes or characteristics and how each will contribute to your goal as a successful professional nurse. Of primary concern would be your problem-solving, interpersonal, and communication skills.

Step 3: Identify your emotional-psychological reactions to the world of nursing. Do not confine yourself to the illustrations in this chapter; include all that you have reviewed to this point.

Step 4: Do you meet the minimum health requirements? Can you rise to the educational demands?

Step 5: Do you really want to be a successful professional nurse? State the reasons for your conclusions. Save your "word image" of a successful nurse for later reference.

Chapter III

The Educational Requirements of a Professional Nurse

The current system of educating professional nurses is being critically evaluated, with plans proposed to restructure the program. Under the present structure, the licensed practical nurse is required to complete a one-year nursing program. After receiving licensure from the state of residence, the LPN provides direct patient care supervised by a registered nurse or a physician. Registered nurses can be graduates of one of three nursing programs: an associate degree, which is a two-year junior college program; a three-year hospital diploma program; or a four-year bachelor of science university program. Interestingly, all three classifications of nurses take identical three-day state boards.

Some structural changes have already been implemented. The three-year diploma program has virtually become extinct. If the new format is adopted, the licensed practical nurse could be phased out or reclassified with distinct professional limitations. The associate degree registered nurse title may be changed, possibly to technical nurse, and the professional responsibilities would be revised accordingly. It is quite possible that the technical nurse would be severely restricted from holding management and other administrative positions.

Even today, after state boards, the differences between levels of education can be significant. All other personal qualities and professional qualifications being equal, the BS nurse probably has the competitive edge. The BS nurse can command a higher salary commensurate with education; managerial and administrative positions are more readily attainable; and career advancement is usually accelerated.

As you read this chapter, remember that high school is the ideal time to determine the educational requirements for admission into the college or university and nursing program of your choice. If you decide *now* which academic requirements you have not met, you can incorporate those classes into your high school curriculum. Enrolling in college preparatory courses is an excellent means of meeting most of your college admission prerequisites.

Before you consult your high school counselor to plan next semester's classes, establish your basic career goals by answering these questions?

- What nursing functions do you want to be engaged in five years from now?
- Are you on the fast track, seeking rapid nursing advancement?
- How much time, money, and energy are you willing to invest in your vocational endeavor?
- Which basic nursing program is tailored to your specific professional aspirations?
- If you opt to start with a two-year associate degree program, will you be able to transfer your credits to a four-year university if you decide to continue your formal education at a later date?
- Which universities will give you credit for your professional clinical (work) experience? In some universities you can CLEP (College Level Examination Program) certain classes; that is, if you pass the exam, you are awarded full credit without taking the course.
- How many credits would you lose because of "old age"? Once credits are six years old, they are generally placed in permanent retirement.

Give serious thought to these two questions: How would you cope with being a student nurse again after enjoying the freedom and responsibilities of a registered nurse? If you hope to advance in a clinical specialty, or climb the administrative ladder, what minimum nursing degree would qualify you for the advancement?

Now is the time to investigate all your options. Talk with several nurses from each area that interests you. Seek out graduates of each of the three types of nursing programs. Ask them open-ended, probing questions. Ask the two-year and three-year graduates if their career aspirations have been thwarted by not having a BS degree. Ask them if a BSN is in their immediate or future plans. If not, what professional action will they take? Ask the BS nurses if they feel the degree really gave them a competitive edge. Talk with nurses who have graduated from various universities and compare the schools of nursing. Which were best prepared for the state boards, and why? Which nurses are the most adept in the working world, and why? Which nursing schools stressed clinical? Which emphasized theory? Who offered the best managerial preparation?

It is your privilege to send letters of inquiry to the universities that interest you. Your efforts can yield valuable data on which to base your decision. Thoroughly read all the information you receive, then carefully weigh all the facts as you compare the positives and negatives of each school against your professional objectives. Consider the advice of the professionals you surveyed. Take into account the dates they graduated. College information more than three years old could be obsolete.

The general university admission requirements are different from the nursing school program. Admission to the university does *not* guarantee admission to the nursing program. Be certain you qualify for entrance to *both*. It is possible to be denied admission to the nursing program until you meet its prerequisites. That could set you back a full year, because nursing is taught in sequence. You must complete Fundamentals of Nursing before you take Medical-Surgical Nursing, and so forth.

A high percentage of institutions of higher learning do check your high school grade point. If your grade point is substandard, make an extra effort to raise it above the minimum required for admission to both the university and school of nursing. Pave your smooth transition from high school through college by recognizing and exceeding standards *before* they become requirements. If you acknowledge and adhere to the university's rules and regulations in advance, you will avoid grave disappointment.

Acceptance for college entrance is a big step. Preparation now could save you valuable time and money as well as embarrassment in the future. The financial burden of chemistry as a high school course is negligible, but at the college level one course could cost you from $50 to $250 or more per credit hour.

General College Admission Procedure

Obtain catalogs of colleges that interest you. Try to make a personal visit to the campus. If your visit proves satisfactory, you should commence the admission process.

Usually the first step is to procure an application for admission from the university. Submit the completed application form, an official copy of your high school transcripts, your ACT (American College Test) or SAT (Scholastic Aptitude Test) results, and any other forms deemed necessary. The vast majority of colleges recommend that high school students submit completed paperwork about one year before planned admission. Early in your senior year, September or October, is best.

After acceptance to the university, you register at a prescribed time. You then meet with your academic advisor, select suitable classes, receive your student ID (identification) card, review your financial status, make housing arrangements, reserve your text-books, tour the campus, and learn the particularities of the school. If you are to live on campus, you will be expected to move into the residence hall at a given time. Most universities offer get-ac-quainted programs for freshmen, before classes begin as well as after.

The following might be your general requirements checklist for college admission.

- Complete your admission application and submit it along with transcripts and SAT or ACT results to the college by October of your senior year. The admissions office will verify your acceptance, usually by letter. You may receive your student ID number at this time. It would behoove you to memorize that number; it is your new name.
- If you are going to live on campus, arrange for your housing early. Finish and submit the paperwork before the specified deadline.
- This step is vital: Consult with your academic advisor. Openly and realistically communicate your needs, concerns, goals, strengths, and weaknesses. The purpose of this meeting is to develop an individualized program to satisfy your specific needs.
- If your budget is tight, check out the financial assistance programs offered through the university. Inquire early for financial aid. If for any reason it is denied, alternate arrange-ments can still be made before classes commence.
- Registering for classes can be a tedious pain in the anatomy, especially if your approach is disorganized and incomplete. Before you register, find out exactly what data are needed,

then prepare your paperwork well in advance. Wear comfortable clothing and shoes. Do not forget essentials like your driver's license and social security number. Mail-in registrations can be done, but not usually on first registration.

After general admission to the university has been confirmed, you proceed to the school of nursing.

Nursing Program Admission Requirements

Outline for yourself the framework of the nursing program. What degree does it confer? How many hours of clinical practicum (patient care practice) and theory (classroom study) are required? Are they taught simultaneously, or does the theory precede the clinical experience? How many clinical hours are assigned to each area of nursing? Remember, the more expertise you acquire as a student nurse, the more self-confident you will be as a professional nurse.

What is the nursing program layout? Is it divided into terms, quarters, or semesters? Does the school schedule a summer break, or must you attend classes year around?

Check the nursing school's idiosyncrasies. One junior college has a mandatory attendance rule; if you miss two clinical sessions in one semester, you are dismissed from that term and must retake those classes the following year. The same college does not allow repeating a failed clinical or theory for one year.

What governing agencies have accredited this college? If you plan to supplement your degree with a clinical specialty, continue your college studies at a later date, or enlist in the armed forces, you must be a graduate of a National League for Nursing–accredited school.

What are the instructors' credentials?

Your general requirements checklist for the school of nursing should resemble this:

- Does this school award a licensed practical nurse certificate, a two-year associate degree, or a four-year bachelor of science in nursing degree?
- What number of hours of clinical and theory in each area of study is required for graduation.
- Outline the program layout.

- List any objectionable idiosyncrasies of the school.
- Confirm the school's accreditation by the National League for Nursing.
- Highlight each instructor's credentials.

You may wish to answer these general questions before making your final decision.

- What is your projected date of admission?
- Is there a waiting list at your favorite university or the corresponding nursing program?
- What criteria are employed in the admission process?
- What is the number of students ahead of you on the waiting list, their grade point, and other influencing credentials?

Even though the LPN program is under scrutiny, it is still available. At this time, the program is offered both in a hospital setting and at junior colleges having external clinical affiliations. Provided the educational and training qualities are adequate, both the hospital and the college curricula are equally functional.

As you review all three nursing programs, note their basic similarities and distinctions.

- What negative or positive factors of each do you consider noteworthy?
- What courses could you take while still in high school to ease your burden in college? Most universities stress math and the natural sciences.
- Does the university or college honor the Transfer or Articulation Agreement? This intercollegiate agreement guarantees that all credits taken at school X, a junior college, may be transferred to school Y, a four-year university.
- Is the nursing program you are considering designed to accommodate educational continuum? That means that successful completion of Level I entitles you to direct entry into Level II without extra admission procedures.

The difference between the Articulation Agreement and the educational continuum is simple. Articulation involves two nursing schools; you transfer from a two-year college to a four-year nursing program. Educational continuum is advancement from

Level I to Level II within the same nursing school system. This program is customarily offered at a junior college, with the LPN being Level I and the associate degree RN constituting Level II.

The virtue of the educational continuum LPN programs is that they meet individual needs, and many are being designed to accommodate legislative restructuring. After completing the one-year LPN program, you can take your state boards and enter the work force or move directly to Level II, the associate degree RN. A second feature of this program is that if after one year's clinical experience you decide to return to nursing school, you can continue where you stopped. In addition, all credits earned in the associate degree program may transfer directly to specified four-year nursing programs through the Articulation Agreement.

If a course is not transferable because of length or other problem, you may be able to use the CLEP option. For a fee, you are permitted to take an examination in the course. If you pass with a 2.0 or better, you are awarded full credit for the course. This option must be investigated; it is not universally available.

The associate degree two-year registered nurse program is one step above the LPN in the hierarchy. Nursing theory and other mandated general courses are taught on campus. Clinical instruction occurs in various external health care delivery settings, from hospitals to doctors' offices.

The top-ranked undergraduate program is the bachelor of science in nursing degree. The first-year curriculum is composed exclusively of basic studies and general humanities. During the sophomore year clinical nursing is integrated into the program.

The outstanding differences between the associate degree and the bachelor of science programs are two. The obvious distinction is length: two years versus four years. The second major difference is in the curriculum. The BS degree offers a broader base of general knowledge than the associate degree.

These are the typical admission requirements of a two-year junior college nursing program.

- After your general admission file is approved by General Admissions, you will be considered a candidate for the school of nursing.
- You will probably be expected to have a health check. Usually a physical, an immunization update, and a dental exam are all that is required.

- Sometimes you must supply written references. Some schools require a personal interview.
- The college may require you to pass an entrance exam.
- You must satisfy financial obligations before admission.
- Before you are accepted into the nursing school, all other prerequisites must be met.
- The grade point required ranges from 2.0 to 4.0. Naturally, the higher grade point, the better your chances of admission.

Four-year BS degree admission requirements are similar.

- General university acceptance is step one.
- Prerequisite classes, if not taken in high school, are completed in the freshman year before entrance to the nursing program in the sophomore year.
- Fairly common grade point requirement is 2.5 to 3.0.
- The preferred academic concentration is mathematics and science.
- Some schools of nursing ask about your health-related vocational experience (nurse's aide or hospital volunteer). This serves the same purpose as references.

Following is an overview of the curricula of each program.

In a typical licensed practical nurse curriculum, you commence with English, Psychology, Growth and Development, Anatomy and Physiology, Nutrition, Pharmacology, Nursing Fundamentals I, classroom theory, and clinical experience. You then take Personal and Community Health with the corresponding theory and clinical, then Medical-Surgical Nursing I, II, and III, with theory and clinical, and finally, Parent and Child Nursing with theory and clinical.

An associate degree program might begin with English, Psychology, Sociology, Anatomy and Physiology I and II, and Nutrition. Add to that Personal and Community Health, Growth and Development, and Pharmacology I, II, and sometimes III. The conventional starting point is Nursing Fundamentals, theory and clinical, followed by Medical-Surgical Nursing I, II and perhaps III; of course, both theory and clinical are taught. The theory and clinical of Parent and Child Nursing, along with Microbiology, Pathophysiology, and Fundamentals of Chemistry may be next. Nursing Role Transition is of major significance. Other nursing courses are

Mental Health, theory and clinical; Parent and Child, advanced theory and clinical; Medical Ethics; Complex Medical-Surgical, clinical and theory; Nursing Management and Trends, and Political Science.

A typical four-year bachelor of science nursing program is as follows:

Freshman year courses are English I and II, Sociology, Chemistry, Literature I and II, Psychology, History, Political Science, and an elective.

During the sophomore year nursing courses begin: Anatomy and Physiology I and II, Fundamentals of Nursing, theory and clinical, and Nursing I, theory and clinical. Nutrition, Pathology, Human Growth and Development, Sociology, and Physical Education I and II are probably added.

During the junior year you study Pharmacology, Nursing I and II with theory and clinical, Microbiology, Health Assessment, and two electives, usually in speech and language.

In the senior year the program is completed with Nursing IV and V, theory and clinical, a philosophy or religion elective, a language elective, and a free elective.

As you approach college admission, do your homework. Know what you need and want.

- Establish your immediate and long-range career goals.
- Talk with active professional nurses.
- Study the school's curriculum. Know in advance the short-comings and how you plan to compensate for each. If your nursing credits will not transfer to a four-year university but the general basic studies will, how will this affect your future plans?
- Prevent unpleasant surprises by being aware of the school's expectations. If chemistry is a prerequisite, take it *before applying* for admission, if at all possible. If you must have a 3.0 grade point average and yours is 2.79, take a few classes that will enrich your nursing studies and raise your grade point above the minimum requirement.
- If your funds are short, apply for financial aid well in advance.
- An alternative if you are short on cash or lack the scholastic aptitude for a four-year university degree is to attend a junior college, raise your grade point, and bank the dollars you save

in tuition fees. That is a plausible solution to some people's financial or academic problems.

Following is a brief description of typical course content.

Human Anatomy and Physiology is the study of anatomical structure and its correlating bodily functions.

Fundamentals of Nursing introduces the basic technical skills and concepts essential to being a professional nurse.

Medical-Surgical Nursing teaches the nurse how to administer personalized nursing care to adult patients with specific medical or surgical problems.

Mental Health Nursing prepares the nurse to identify a mentally stable patient's psychological needs, while providing individualized care to patients exhibiting behavioral abnormalities.

Family and the Neonate Nursing covers Obstetrics and care of the mother and newborn.

Nursing of Children encompasses growth and development of the pediatric patient, focusing on the needs of both the ill and well child.

Introduction to Managerial Skills is self-explanatory. Often included in this course are planning, organizing, and implementing the nursing care plan.

Trends in Nursing examines the legal, personal, social, economic, and external forces affecting nurses.

Pharmacology instructs nurses in the use of physician-prescribed therapeutic drugs. Courses may include administration techniques, specific therapeutic action of the medication, and individual variances in physiological response.

Financial Assistance Programs Available to Nursing Students

Financial assistance programs have slight variances, but the major points are universal. All should be applied for well in advance. The programs are plentiful, but eligibility requirements may be rigid.

Study each institution's financial assistance programs. What type of aid does your school offer—work-study, grants, loans? If you are contemplating a student loan, is there a ceiling? What are the terms of repayment and the interest rate? What are the eligibility requirements? Does the school issue or honor grants?

Who is eligible for a grant? Are there grounds on which it must be repaid? Are scholarships issued? What are the eligibility requirements? Who grants scholarships? Are there scholastic achievement stipulations? What work-study programs are offered through the school?

Assess your personal financial resources, and calculate your projected assets and expenses. Then total your fees, including entrance and class fees, the less obvious lab fees, and one-time-only student activities fees. What living arrangements are you making? is the school commutable from home? Will you live in a dorm? Does the cost of the dorm include food? What are parking arrangements? Must you pay for the parking permit in a lump sum, or can you use the installment plan? Count the fringes, too. Will you have a phone bill to contend with? If you are long-winded, that could be a deficit. What is your budgeted weekly allowance for nonessentials? Do you have the financial resources to meet your needs, or should you seek assistance?

Financial assistance programs fall into four primary groups: loans, grants, scholarships, and work-study programs. Each category has a multitude of subdivisions. Seek knowledgeable assistance if you need help in deciphering them. Thoroughly investigate all the alternatives before making your selection.

Scholarships can differ greatly from one institution to another. Scholarships are awarded to qualified nursing students by their school or by a professional nursing organization. Some community organizations sponsor a nursing student, or the Department of Nursing Education may provide funding. Scholarship recipients must demonstrate financial need and scholastic achievement and abide by standards stipulated by the awarding agency. Scholarships do not have to be repaid.

Loans are of numerous types;however, you will become acquainted with only two. The first is the *guaranteed student loan*, which is made by a bank, a credit union, or a savings and loan association and is backed by the government. It has a low interest rate. The second type of loan, the National Direct Student Loan, is more difficult to obtain. This, too, is at a low interest rate, approved, and granted through the institution. Recipients must demonstrate financial hardship. If you are having difficulty finding a lender, consult your state guarantee program. That is your best source of information on student loans.

Grants are federally funded monies awarded to eligible recipients based on several factors, including financial need. You must be a U.S. citizen and live in the United States. The Pell Grant Program (basic education opportunity grant) is the most common. Grants do not have to repaid.

Work-study programs are provided by the institution to help with financial obligations. They offer part-time (20 hours or less per week) on-campus employment. If the on-campus opportunities are limited or unsatisfactory, most campuses list off-campus employment prospects.

Resources for Continuing Education and Specialty Training

Continuing education courses for nurses are offered at many places, including but not limited to colleges, hospitals, organizations, and nursing associations.

Specialty training, both formal and informal, is offered at select universities, some hospitals, and nursing organizations established to meet the needs of a particular specialty.

Postgraduate health care studies are available at most universities.

Your best sources of information are your high school counselor, the State Board of Nursing Licensing and Regulation Department, the library, and the National League for Nursing.

Panic! It is time for your state boards. In order to take the exam, you must graduate from a nursing school, file an application for licensure, and pay the fee. State boards are given several times each year. They are administered, proctored, and controlled by the individual State Licensing and Regulation Board. The exam is divided into sections; it is completed over a three-day period for RN's and one day for LPN's.

The best foundation you can lay for passing the state boards is to learn as you go. Last-minute review can be a valuable refresher, but last-minute cramming is an exercise in futility. You must have a working knowledge of steps A and B before F and G make sense. A little extra effort now is your insurance against misery later.

Reader's Review

Which of the three nursing programs will you investigate? Which type of program meets your current needs? Which type will most likely meet your needs six to ten years from now?

How will you make the transition?

Do you prefer to secure your primary education all at once or ride the educational continuum?

If you are serious about making progress in nursing, strongly consider the bachelor of science in nursing degree. Although abundant nursing opportunities are available to all nurses, you may still find some major roadblocks to advancement or diversification without the bachelor's degree. Certain fields of nursing require a BS to be a field nurse. It is mandatory for management and for nurse clinicians, except in rare cases.

You may save valuable time later by investing four years now. Some nurses, because of transfer problems, have earned degrees in related fields. That may or may not meet your needs. Check first to secure your place at the top. *Before* enrolling in any program, ascertain whether all your credits will transfer to a four-year university, even if you have no intention of earning a bachelor's degree.

The following are case histories of three nurses who have climbed their ladder. None of the three has a BS. However, note the formal education each must now complete to continue or advance from their present status.

Chris Bekish, RN, has a diploma in nursing. She has served as an inservice director, a director of nursing services, and is now administrator of a nursing home. Chris has passed her administrator's training and exam. She is obliged to complete 19 c.e.u.'s (continuing education units) per year to maintain her license.

Carlene Smith, RN, is also a diploma nurse. She is employed by a rural hospital as inservice director and assistant director of nursing services. Carlene is actively working toward her bachelor of science in nursing. She has been a registered nurse for twelve years.

Jackie Heron, RN, graduated from an associate degree program and has performed the duties of inservice director and director of nursing services for a home health agency, a hospital, and a nursing home. She is the founder and owner of her own health care consulting service. Jackie is actively pursuing a degree in health administration and has passed her nursing home administrator's board. She has been a professional for fourteen years.

Many nurses of our era had no intention of future studies, but professional obligations and new legislation have demanded further education to maintain their present status or advance. Many nurses who graduated ten or more years ago have virtually had to start from square one to obtain degrees. You have multiple educational opportunities laid out in front of you. Use them to honor your career goals; do not lose them.

Chapter IV

Nursing as a Lifetime Career

Plan Your Career Goals and Strategies

A successful nurse views nursing as a life-style, not an occupational stepping-stone. You are embarking on a profession in transition, one that is fast-paced and technologically advancing. Successful nurses are constantly making changes in their personal and professional lives to create a positive life-style. This is accomplished by resolving minor discrepancies between home and career before a crisis arises. How do you achieve this? Quite simply; you stay in touch with yourself and "significant others," like your immediate family. Be open to constantly restructure both career and private life to meet family and vocational requirements.

As a professional nurse, you control your own destiny and set your own restrictions. Those restrictions are primarily influenced by the degree of educational preparation you pursue and the level of professional, technical, and clinical expertise you achieve. Other dominant factors are the personal resources you invest, the flexibility with which you function, the direct application of your interpersonal skills, and your creativity and ability to adapt to change.

Analyze the following situations from your perspective now, and again at the end of the chapter. Will your answers change?

You have been a Gerontology nurse for thirteen years, ten of them at the same facility. The veteran director of nursing services retires and is replaced. Within a month, the new director introduces a new type of charting, effective immediately. While you are still coping with the first dilemma, she abruptly informs the staff that all patient care data will be computerized within three months, beginning next week.

Your education is limited to one year of hospital training as a licensed practical nurse in an educational continuum, or stepladder program. Your clinical expertise has been achieved by experience.

Your continuing education has been limited to the inservices provided in-house. The personal resources you have invested are thirteen years of clinical experience in Gerontology. You have voluntarily worked overtime when there were staff shortages.

In your personality analysis, you highlight your assets. Your interpersonal skills are excellent, but you realize that you could exercise more patience with paraprofessionals. Your creativity is limited, and you sometimes need to employ other professional resources. You are reasonably flexible and able to compromise but your adaptation to change is slower than it should be.

Your general assessment is that you have enjoyed your tenure at this long-term-care facility. You also realize that thirteen years is a significant investment of time.

In light of the above information, what would you do if you were this nurse? What is your rationale for your reaction?

- Would you discuss the rapidity of the changes being sought with other nurses, the administrator, the new director of nurses?
- Would you complain to other nurses, but do nothing to present your thoughts to the new director?
- Would you quietly put forth additional effort to learn the new computer and charting systems?
- Would you quit and go where you hope technology will not find you?

Only you know what you would really do! Not what you should do or could do, but what you *would* do. Those answers say a lot about you. Think what each one means.

The following is a case history of a successful nurse who coordinated career and personal objectives to maintain a harmonious lifestyle.

Leslie G. graduated from an LPN program and accepted employment at a metropolitan hospital (450 beds). While there, she specialized in Gynecology. After a year and a half she was unable to gain a promotion, so she resigned.

Her next step was a large university teaching institute. Shortly after her orientation was complete, domestic responsibilities created chaos in her life. Unable to satisfy both work and home demands, she chose to restructure her career to restore harmony.

She accepted a position as a home health care nurse and gave excellent patient care, utilizing current technical skills along with her interpersonal skills, common sense, and personal preference for one-on-one patient care. An important fact to remember is that nursing skills are cumulative and transferable from one nursing situation to another. You can build on your present skills to meet ultimate expectations.

In less than a year, family circumstances forced a residence relocation that necessitated a job change. Formal education had not prepared Leslie for Cardiac Care; however, a personal assessment revealed that many of her present clinical skills and personality traits would help fill the vacuum until she could acquire the education to solidify her position. The birth of her son created a conflict between home and career. To cope with this dilemma, she elected to restructure her career. She began her own medical supply business.

Notice the progression from staff nurse to her own business. A strong basic foundation of clinical skills was continually added to. Her personality talents prepared her to cope effectively with changes on the career and home fronts. Combined clinical expertise and personal attributes facilitated upward mobility. At present, Leslie is pursuing a bachelor's in health administration and has taken the nursing home administrator's boards. She restructured her career as her needs changed; hence, her nursing career is a satisfying and successful life-style.

Next is the story of Carlene Smith, a three-year diploma graduate. Carlene has worked at the same 42-bed acute-care hospital for twelve years, advancing from staff nurse to relief charge nurse, to inservice director and assistant director of nurses. Her continuing education, which facilitated her promotions, was limited to external seminars and workshops. At present, Carlene is anticipating future educational demands for the nursing profession. Before a BSN becomes mandatory, she is seeking her degree at an accredited college. Carlene remains employed full time as assistant director of nursing and inservice director while attending college. Oh, and one other obligation to note: she is also rearing her two-year-old and four-year-old sons.

Obviously, the fewer external obligations you have, the easier it is to acquire the training you desire. However, if you have the ambition and perseverance, the nursing profession has many rewards.

Which Fields of Nursing Appeal to You?

After you have read this section, you will have to do a little serious introspection regarding your personal preferences. Let your intuition be your guide. To eliminate as many variables and generalities as possible, this section discusses only the conventional patient-care units of a medium-sized (300- to 500-bed) hospital.

Here are some general questions you might wish to answer before considering the specifics. What age group of people do you enjoy most? What are your unspoken fears? Do you prefer to work with men or women? That could have a definite effect on your professional preferences. Do you like a fast pace? Are you easily bored? Are you a fast thinker? Can you independently follow through and complete a project within a given time? Do you like working with sophisticated equipment? Do you feel comfortable with routine, or do you prefer rapid change? Do you like to help others? Are you in nursing for the financial rewards? Does working with, listening to, and helping others have a negative impact on you? Can you interpret another's feelings and messages through observation? Do people with visible physical, mental, or emotional handicaps make you self-conscious or uncomfortable? Do you have a lot of patience? Would you be inclined to become depressed if your patient did not recuperate? Do you like working with other people? Does a crying child upset you? Does a child's temper tantrum bother you? Can you keep it together while a patient is throwing up, coughing up phlegm, or suffering with loose stools? Are you oversensitive? Do you take offense at words spoken in haste or anger?

Think about your answers as you read the remainder of the section. Be sure to respond with your "gut" feelings and not your obligatory feelings, lest you defeat your own purpose.

The *unit* is Alcohol and Substance Abuse.

The primary *purpose of hospitalization* is to help a patient through a crisis and then to help him or her discover ways to function without chemical dependency.

The *general function* of the unit is to admit a patient while in the acute phase of abuse and observe him or her closely and accurately for adverse physiological, psychological, emotional, and mental reactions. Common observations include the symptoms of withdrawal, inappropriate social behavior, tremors, hallucinations, and fluid and electrolytic imbalance. After the acute phase, counseling and therapy are given for the duration of the stay.

The *floor nurse's responsibilities* are to prevent untoward reactions during the acute phase. When the acute phase has subsided, counseling and therapy are designed to help the patient prevent substance abuse.

The *dress code* for this unit is relaxed and natural. Duplication of the home environment permits the patient to feel comfortable and able to relate to the staff.

What is the *best personality type* to work this unit? A nurse with excellent interpersonal skills is always in demand. Compassion, empathy, a nonjudgmental attitude, patience, and comprehension of the patient's total environment are mandatory qualities. Highly desirable is the ability to function as a member of an interdisciplinary team, contributing pertinent facts while utilizing information received.

The *specialized training* required to work a Substance Abuse Unit varies from one employer to the next. Generally, it is informal training consisting of in-house inservices and external seminars, combined with on-the-job training.

Could you successfully work this unit? Could you effectively care for a repeat offender over a long period of time (often six weeks or more each time)? Do you become impatient with people who "won't help themselves"? Could you contribute to the interdisciplinary team in developing a therapeutic regime in-house and after discharge? Do you have empathy for this problem?

Your earning potential for this unit is an average base of $20,000, plus the variables.

Your earning potential in nursing is on the rise. At this time, salary can range from $20,000 to over $50,000 with the entry-level median being $22,000 to $24,000. Location plays a role in determining salary range. The East Coast pays more than the South, and the Midwest usually pays higher salaries than the West. If you work in a rural setting, chances are good that you will make less than your equal in a metropolitan setting. Odd shifts, second and third, consistently receive a percentage more per hour than their day counterparts, and a premium is paid for holidays, overtime, and weekends. Your level of expertise can elevate your wages. Some institutions pay a bonus for experience, and the majority give financial rewards in accordance with your nursing degree or continuing education. Specially trained nurses receive extra pay, as do those who advance to certification. For the sake of discussion, a base salary of $22,000 plus shift differential, holidays, overtime, a BSN and certification could add as much as $10,000.

The *unit* is Psychiatric.

The primary *purpose of hospitalization* for the patients is to regain mental, emotional, and psychological stability.

The *general function* of the unit is to create a therapeutic environment that will foster normal activities of daily living for the emotionally, mentally, or psychologically unstable or ill person.

The *floor nurse's responsibilities* are to help the patient establish a routine for self-care and to restore self-esteem while dealing with personal problems realistically. As a nurse, you identify the psychological needs of patients who exhibit abnormal behavior or have difficulty in interpersonal relationships.

The *dress code* for this unit is relaxed, in an attempt to duplicate the situation in which the person will ultimately function. Both nurse and patient usually wear street clothes.

What is the *best personality type* to work this unit? Psychiatric nurses must be very secure, self-confident, and aware of their personal holistic status at all times. Psychiatric patients may draw you into their world of make-believe if your personal integrity lapses. You must be psychologically tuned in on all channels at all times. If abnormal behavior disturbs you, this unit may not be your best choice.

The *specialized training* required tends to be informal, consisting of specialized classes taught by the employer or external seminars.

Could you successfully work this unit? Do you like to help people with problems, even if they do not always make sense to you? Do you have lots of patience, empathy, and compassion? Do you excel in people and social skills? Do you have the ability to establish and maintain rapport in a therapeutic milieu? Are you psychologically strong and capable of sorting fact from fantasy? Don't laugh! Some patients' fantasies sound true-to-life. If you are gullible, you will probably be on a tour of the castle in the sky before you realize you have left the ground. Are you able to evaluate readiness for counseling? Are you able to help people accept and deal with overwhelming problems? Are you secure around people who are not quite "with it"? Are you alert to subtle personality changes? Timely intervention may avert crisis intervention.

Your earning potential for this unit averages $20,000 plus the previously discussed variables. An interesting note: If you are a state employee for this unit, your pay could be a little higher.

The *unit* is Neonate (newborn nursery), where infants are kept from birth until discharge.

The primary *purpose of hospitalization* is to identify and correct congenital anomalies, if possible, facilitating the best possible start in life for each child.

The *general function* of the unit is to provide a safe environment for the infant.

The *floor nurse's responsibilities* are multiple. Assessment and observing and recording of pertinent data can easily be incorporated into the physical care of the infant. Teaching the new mother how to care for her newborn, and encouraging bonding between mother, infant, father, and siblings from the moment of birth, are two other outstanding responsibilities.

The *dress code* for this unit is usually scrubs.

What is the *best personality type* to work this unit? A soft disposition and a strong maternal instinct are your shining qualities.

The *specialized training* required is informal and on-the-job.

Could you successfully work this unit? Do you like to hold and cuddle babies? Do you like to teach mothers infant care? Can you respond quickly if an infant begins to choke? Are your observations accurate?

Your earning potential for this unit is the standard base, plus variables.

The *unit* is Labor and Delivery. The primary *purpose of hospitalization* is to monitor mother and infant during labor and birth of the baby. You would intervene medically only to prevent complications for mother or infant.

The *general function* of the unit is to care for a laboring mother and her unborn baby while providing a safe delivery process for her.

The *floor nurse's responsibilities* are typically to monitor, record, and report progress of mother and infant throughout labor and to assist the physician during delivery.

The *dress code* for this unit is hospital scrubs.

What is the *best personality type* to work this unit? A stable, easygoing disposition works admirably. Lots of empathy and the ability to respond appropriately are excellent qualifications.

The *specialized training* required is informal and determined by the individual unit.

Could you successfully work this unit? Does watching someone in pain give you negative vibrations? Can you control your reactions to an abnormal labor or delivery? How would you react to an abnormal infant? *Control does not mean NOT REACTING. It means reacting tactfully as the circumstances dictate.* Are you genuinely interested in new mothers and babies?

Your earning potential for this unit is the standard base, plus variables.

The *unit* is Postpartum.

The primary *purpose of hospitalization* is care of the mother following the birth of her baby.

The *general function* of the unit is to foster mother-child bonding and facilitate recovery of the mother.

The *floor nurse's responsibilities* are to observe the infant-family bonding process and intercede only as needed.

The *dress code* for this unit is scrubs.

What is the *best personality type* to work this unit? A happy, easy-flowing disposition, with a genuine interest in the well-being of mother and infant are necessary attributes. The nurse should enjoy teaching, communicating, and listening and not be bored by routine.

The *specialized training* required is usually informal and determined by the individual unit.

Could you successfully work this unit? Does routine bore you? Do you enjoy teaching? Do you excel in interpersonal skills? Do you enjoy new mothers and babies? You could if you answered yes to those four questions.

Your earning potential for this unit is the standard base, plus variables.

The *unit* is Geriatric Nursing. These nurses care for senior citizens who are acutely ill.

The primary *purpose of hospitalization* is to stabilize or cure a condition and return the patient to his or her state of normalcy.

The *floor nurse's responsibilities* are to administer large doses of supportive therapy while giving direct patient care. Teaching this group of patients and their family members preventive medicine is extremely important. Arranging for care after discharge, when applicable, is also critical.

The *general function* of the unit is specialized care of the geriatric patient.

The *dress code* is usually the classic uniform.

What is the *best personality type* to work this unit? An abundance of empathy and patience are definite assets. Then add an extra measure of tender loving care, a slower pace, and the ability to meet the patient's basic needs for nutrition, shelter, and love. A quiet disposition, flexibility, and adaptability are useful traits.

The *specialized training* required is usually informal and designed to meet the individual unit's needs.

Could you successfully work this unit? Can you comfortably work at a slower pace, permitting a patient as much independence as

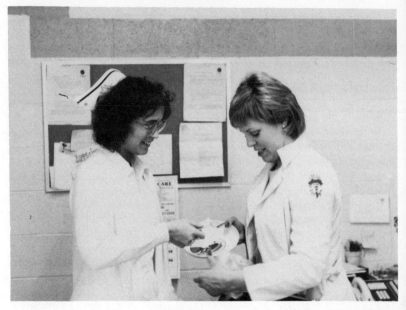

COURTESY BEVERLY MANOR
An RN discusses a patient's new equipment with an ROT (Registered Occupational Therapist).

possible? Are you capable of fostering self-esteem by supportive direction and guidance, not control? Do you enjoy older people?

Your earning potential for this unit is the base salary plus the common variables. If it is a nursing home setting, the pay could be less than in an acute-care setting.

The *unit* is Pediatrics and the Family.

The primary *purpose of hospitalization* is to care for the ill child.

The *general function* of the unit is to preserve the child's mental and physical integrity while in the hospital, taking into account the effects the child's hospitalization has on the family unit.

The *floor nurse's responsibilities* are to meet the child's and family's emotional needs while providing nursing care. Teaching the family and child restorative measures and preventive maintenance is important.

The *dress code* for this unit is usually colored uniforms.

What is the *best personality type* to work this unit? Strong father or mother imagery, with love and understanding of children. Kids need lots of tender loving care. Safety awareness and accident prevention are of paramount importance.

The *specialized training* required is ordinarily informal, on-the-job training.

Could you successfully work this unit? Do you like children? Can you cope with nonstop crying for mommy? Can you deal with behavioral problems?

Your earning potential for this unit is the standard base plus variables.

The *unit* is the Operating room.

The primary *purpose of hospitalization* is surgery. A patient elects to have a specific surgical procedure performed to relieve or eliminate a physical malady.

The *general function* of the unit is to maintain an aseptic, anesthetic environment, conducive to safe surgical procedures, and to control all aspects of each operation.

The *floor nurse's responsibilities* are dual. One nurse circulates and delivers surgical supplies to each surgical suite, as needed. Other nurses stand at the operating table to hand appropriate instruments to the physician.

The *dress code* for this unit is hospital scrubs.

What is the *best personality type* to work this unit? One who enjoys working with equipment and physicians and monitoring an anesthetized patient's status would be an excellent candidate.

The *specialized training* required is particular to each unit.

Could you successfully work this unit? Do you like working with instruments? Can you stand for long periods of time? Are your hands steady?

Your earning potential for this unit is more than base, because it is a specialty unit.

The *unit* is Recovery Room.

The *general function* of the unit is to monitor a postsurgical patient until he or she is completely reactive from the anesthesia. This includes monitoring vital signs until stable and noting untoward postsurgical reactions.

The *floor nurse's responsibilities* are to constantly assess, monitor, record, and evaluate each patient's level of consciousness and vital signs. Guarding against the specific complications associated with a particular surgery is extremely important.

The *dress code* for this unit is scrubs.

What is the *best personality type* to work this unit? One who is quick to observe very minute changes, either physical or mental; one who enjoys observing changes in another person's physical and mental status.

The *specialized training* required is determined by the hospital.

Could you successfully work this unit? Do you react quickly? Do you tolerate stress well? Are your observational skills keen? Can you deal effectively with a wide range of possible complications? Do minor inconveniences like vomiting upset you?

Your earning potential for this unit is a little higher base than some units. Recovery Room is considered a specialty in most hospitals.

The *unit* is Emergency Room.

The primary *purpose of hospitalization* is to correct or stabilize a life-threatening problem. Patient may or may not be admitted as an inpatient.

The *general function* of the unit is to deal directly with life-threatening physical problems.

The *floor nurse's responsibilities* are to rapidly assess, evaluate, and respond with immediate action to prevent or inhibit death.

The *dress code* for this unit can be a uniform or scrubs, as determined by the hospital.

What is the *best personality type* to work this unit? You should be energetic, organized, calm under pressure, and possess excellent observational skills. Being adept at following doctors' orders, having good hand coordination, and being able to assess physical, mental, emotional, and psychological states are mandatory.

The *specialized training* required is planned by the individual unit.

Could you successfully work this unit? Can you cope with four major crises occurring simultaneously? Can you absorb and follow doctors' oral directives in succession? Can you tolerate high stress? Can you handle three simultaneous admissions and then a three-hour block without any? Do you know your own limitations?

Your earning potential for this unit is base, plus variables. However, many institutions consider the Emergency room a specialty unit and offer higher pay.

The *unit* is general Medical. This hospital wing houses patients with medical ailments. A larger hospital (200 or more beds) usually groups patients with like disorders on the same unit, for ease of care and organization. A small rural hospital (less than 100 beds) may elect to combine all medical patients on one unit.

The primary *purpose of hospitalization* is treatment of any physical illness not requiring surgical intervention to correct or stabilize.

The *general function* of the unit is to treat and correct problems that create bodily malfunctions and prohibit normal activity. This is accomplished with medications or other forms of nonsurgical treatment.

The *unit* is general Surgical. It houses patients who will undergo surgery to correct a physical problem.

The primary *purpose of hospitalization* is to correct a bodily malfunction by use of invasive techniques.

The *general function* of the unit is to prepare the patient physically, psychologically, emotionally, and mentally for the Operating Room, to assure the patient a safe and uncomplicated surgical procedure. Then, postsurgically, to assure the patient of an uneventful recovery.

The *floor nurse's responsibilities* are many. Excellent observation and assessment skills are imperative, as well as monitoring the patient carefully and frequently for changes in medical, physical, emotional, and psychological status. Carrying out physician's orders implicitly is of paramount importance. You must plan, write, and implement the individualized nursing-care plan. A supplemental duty would be to instruct patients and family in the intricacies of the illness and preventive maintenance.

The *dress code* for this unit is a uniform. Hospital policy dictates the details of color and style.

What is the *best personality type* to work this unit? You must be detail-oriented and possess physical fortitude. The observations, charting, inservicing, and doctors' orders require an abundance of detailed work. Sometimes the physical work is heavy. Good concentration, accuracy, good listening skills, and a desire for a challenge are positive personal attributes.

The *specialized training* required is usually informal and determined by each unit.

Could you successfully work this unit? If someone vomits, do you lose it? Can you react quickly if someone begins to faint? Are your organizational, observational, and assessment skills adequate? Can you follow long, complex, and sometimes tedious physicians' orders flawlessly?

Your earning potential for this unit is base, plus extra specialty

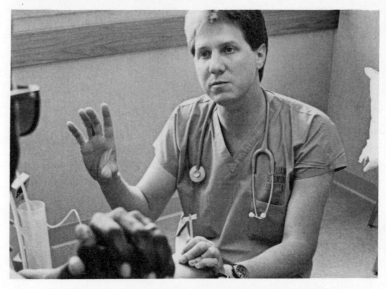

COURTESY WILLIAM BEAUMONT HOSPITAL
An RN explains procedures to a patient.

certifications, and the common variables. Listed below are the common areas of division for medical and surgical units, accompanied by basic characteristics of each.

Orthopedics corrects musculoskeletal problems. Requirements for this unit include lots of heavy lifting and positioning of patients. Good body mechanics are essential. These patients are often immobile for long periods of time. Large doses of tender loving care decrease anxiety.

The *Gynecology* floor takes care of women with disorders of the female organs. Assets include being a good listener, having empathy, and offering enthusiastic encouragement to accompany your professional technical skills.

The *Cardiac* or *Coronary Care Unit* deals with patients with cardiovascular problems. Some patients may be young, but the conventional CCU admits middle-aged and up. This is a fast-paced, high-stress unit, with lots of sophisticated equipment. Snap lifesaving decisions are demanded frequently. You must be rational, a quick thinker, and quick to respond.

An *Intensive Care unit* requires characteristics like those of

Cardiac Care. The patients in this unit are critically ill and require nonstop monitoring.

Urology is the treatment of patients with urinary tract ailments. Medication, IV's, measuring and recording intake and output, interpreting diagnostic lab studies, and monitoring patients for signs and symptoms of fluid-electrolyte imbalance are common tasks.

The *Thoracic* floor houses patients with ailments of the chest. Everything from chest tubes to upper respiratory infections are distinct possibilities. As in all units, isolation is employed for contagious diseases.

A *Gastrointestinal Tract Unit (GI)* treats patients having digestive system ailments. Common problems for you to face could be patients suffering from nausea, vomiting, and diarrhea. A fluid-electrolyte imbalance can cause dehydration, which in turn can result in a temporary personality disorder that you must spot. If surgical treatment is rendered, colostomies and appendectomies are two possibilities.

Metabolic disorders, malfunctions of the body's metabolism, are often integrated with other medical conditions. Diabetes mellitus is a common example.

Dermatology nurse is treatment of skin disorders. Patients are usually admitted to a general Medical Unit.

Treatment of *Cancer* victims can be depressing. It is imperative that you thoroughly comprehend the rationale for all treatments and be able to cope with death and dying.

Neurological disorders are problems of the nervous system, ranging from brain tumors to seizures. Empathy, patience, and a positive attitude are critical to successful nursing in this unit.

Is Your Preference General or Specialty Nursing?

Whether you choose to be a nurse generalist or a clinical nurse specialist depends upon your personality and preferences. Even though there is a tendency to specialization, generalists are still very much in demand.

As a rule, nurse generalists thrive in a rural setting, and clinical specialists are in great demand on the suburban-urban front. Nurse generalists may work on a general Medical Unit treating a variety of medical conditions, including diabetes, skin disorders, and seizure patients.

Nurse specialists, on the contrary, concentrate on one type of disorder in a specialty unit. For instance, a patient suffering from a cardiovascular disorder would be admitted to CCU or Cardiac Care. There are arguments on both sides of being a generalist or a specialist. Some say that the generalist cannot know all there is to know about everything and wonder if that nurse will know what to do if an unusual complication arises. To counter, others say that special-ists are too limited, with their knowledge concentrated in only one area.

Both arguments are right and wrong. No one can know all there is to know about an illness. A good nurse generalist, however, observes patients closely and keeps accurate records of their condition. Then the nurse deduces the cause of any changes and contacts the physician for further instructions if necessary. On the contrary, nurse specialists prepare in the best way possible to meet their professional obligations and the needs of their patients. Who is right and who is wrong depends upon your personal and career aspirations.

Frequently, nurses are required to complete extensive, intensive classroom and clinical study before being permitted to work a specialty unit. Four universally recognized specialty units are Emergency Room, Operating Room, Intensive Care, and Cardiac Care. Patients in any of these units are usually clinically unstable and often in a life-or-death situation.

If the challenge and financial rewards appeal to you, and you want to specialize, the next question you must answer is "What level of specialization?" You can choose your level of specialization, ranging from certification to graduate-level clinical specialist.

You can also specialize in an area that is not a specialty unit. For instance, if you choose Gynecology, your training will most likely be informal and designed to meet specific unit standards. You can work on the unit for a certain period of time, pass written and clinical requirements that are certified by letters of reference, and receive membership in the specialty organization. You can advance up the ladder another rung by taking your certification exam to be a nurse clinician or nurse practitioner if this specialty interests you. At this time you are not required to have a certification to work the unit. Naturally, if you become certified, it will be reflected in your paycheck.

If you choose Cardiac Care, a designated specialty unit, you will be required to take formal specialty classes at a college or university. After a specified period of clinical experience, usually two years, and clinical exams, you will be eligible to attend Cardiac Care Nurse Certification training and take the certification boards. Master's-level graduate studies would advance you to nurse clinician or nurse practitioner.

Well, which do you want to be? A nurse generalist capable of caring for a variety of illnesses with superior excellence, or a nurse specialist dealing exclusively with patients having one kind of illness? Do not make any snap decisions. Consider your personality traits, then talk with nurse generalists, specialty nurses in a nonspecialty area, and finally specialty nurses working in a high-stress specialty unit.

Do You Prefer Patient Care, Teaching, or Management?

Before you decide to bypass direct patient care and sit in the director of nurses chair, remember that patient care is the primary reason we are nurses. Patient care is the central theme and substance of the professional nurse. You cannot, and should not, bypass patient care to excel at teaching or management. You must first comprehend the theory and perfect your clinical skills through patient care. This learning experience will give you the working knowledge you need to manage unanticipated happenings in nursing. To take care of patients and guide and direct other health care personnel, you must first have had similar experiences. Before you can really teach someone, you must first have had hands-on experience. You must care about and like people before you can project the proper attitude and feelings to others.

Management and teaching positions (frequently referred to as administrative and inservice, respectively) usually require at least a BS degree and sometimes an advanced degree. Managerial positions always require clinical expertise in the area. You could not be head nurse on a CCU if you could not conduct a code (cardiopulmonary resuscitation); you could not teach staff nurses how to start IV's if you could not do it yourself. A strong foundation in direct patient care, while increasing your professional knowledge and technical skills, assures you of your choice of nursing positions.

Suppose you feel or know that you are better suited to teaching, or administration, than direct patient care.

As a practicing staff nurse, you teach patients and their loved ones all the time. You demonstrate managerial expertise in your mini-world. To help yourself advance, capitalize on your proven talents and perfect your less-than-perfect skills. During inservices you attend, pay particular attention to effective and ineffective teaching techniques. Ask yourself these questions: Do you speak clearly? Do you maintain eye contact? Do you comprehend and apply readiness levels to learning? Can you alter your lesson plan at a minute's notice? Can you teach on the level of the learner?

Patient Inservice Coordinator. Individual patient-care teaching is a task for all nurses. However, some hospitals employ nurses whose primary function is to teach patients details about their health problem. Inservice coordinators are usually expected to have advanced training and/or graduate training. Advanced training in this case refers to a BSN minimum. Patients are given classes tailored to their specific needs.

Personnel Inservice Coordinator. This nurse's primary responsibility is to teach nursing personnel new procedures and keep their skill levels updated. Educational requirements for personnel inservice coordinators are compatible with Patient Inservice Personnel.

Health Educator. The term health educator encompasses professionals teaching health care on several levels. To teach people to be nursing assistants, a BS and certification would probably suffice. To teach an associate degree nursing program, a BS would be a minimum requirement, and quite likely inadequate to secure a position unless you were actively pursuing a master's. To teach in a BS nursing program, a master's would be the minimum and you would probably need a PhD. Health educators work in many areas, including industry and consulting. Their educational requirements are established by the employers.

Suppose you are a leader and are seeking a *health care management* position. Contemplate these factors before you make a final commitment. As a manager, your time and most of your life belong to your employer. You are on 24-hour call and responsible for all nursing activities whether you are on the premises or not. Even if your assistant or designee takes calls for you, you are accountable for each decision rendered and the outcome.

Do you cope well with this type of pressure? Are you truly a good leader? Are you adept at problem-solving? Are you approachable? Can you communicate effectively? Do you like being held accountable for another's behavior? When things go smoothly, you get credit. When the bottom falls out, you are the target.

A good manager cannot sit in an office and delegate responsibilities. This is a highly visible position, and you must be available to talk with the nurses when the need arises. You must understand the problems each nurse faces and be able to offer feasible suggestions and support. You should be a good decision-maker, one who gathers and implements team input to arrive at a solution. Then you should employ team feedback to determine its effectiveness.

Management on any level almost certainly requires a bachelor of science degree or being in pursuit of one. When the situation requires, you must be able to exercise clinical and managerial skills as well as sound judgment.

The following description of responsibilities and corporate structure is a general delineation; the chain of command may vary from one organization to the next. In this summary, charge nurses are not included in management.

Assistant head nurse and *head nurse* are considered entry-level management. The assistant head nurse can work any shift. She shares responsibility for her unit's level of patient care and is expected to contribute to administrative decisions. The assistant head nurse reports to the head nurse. A head nurse is responsible for all nursing functions on her unit 24 hours per day. She reports to the shift supervisor.

The *shift supervisor* is responsible for all nurses from all units on her shift. This includes all hospital functions involving the nursing staff and patients. The shift supervisor usually reports to the assistant director of nurses.

The *assistant director of nursing* and the *director of nursing* are at the top of the nursing management ladder. The director of nursing is responsible for all nursing and business functions, as well as patient care, and reports to the administrator. (The administrator runs the hospital.) The director of nursing makes all decisions involving the nurses and is well versed on all upcoming professional and institutional changes affecting her division. The assistant director of nurses is delegated specific responsibilities by the director of nursing. In the absence of the director of nursing, the assistant director of nurses becomes the acting director of nursing.

Management in all health organizations involves clinical and business expertise. So you want to be the boss, run the show. Can you motivate others? Are you a good listener? Are you empathic? Can you adapt to change while assisting those who will not? Can you accurately assess "total" situations? Are you judgmental or biased? Can you work well with others? Good nursing managers establish a support system and a network. Are you capable of structuring your own?

Here is a minor but typical problem for the director of nursing of a small acute-care hospital. Your scheduled workday is 9:00 a.m. to 5:00 p.m. You consistently arrive half an hour early, and it is not uncommon for you to leave fifteen minutes to half an hour late by the time you meet second shift's needs. On this particular night you arrive home at 6:30 p.m. At 8:30 the charge nurse calls to inform you that a physician has admitted a "hot" cardiac patient to the unit. The patient is on the monitor and respirator, and your charge nurse has inadequate staff to cover this emergency. Furthermore, midnight staffing will be even tighter because of two call-ins. After you have pulled your hair out, what do you do? First, you check staffing and call all available qualified staff to see if anyone can help cover tonight. There is a catch: You must do it without depleting your other shifts. Remember, state regulations dictate staffing requirements. No one is available. Guess who is elected? That's right, you are it! Realizing that you have three meetings you must attend the next day, you call another nurse to assist you by administering nonregulated drugs and taking and recording vital signs. As expected, the patient codes. You contact the chief of staff, who comes in to conduct the resuscitation, which is successful. During your postcrisis discussion, you explain your staffing problem to him. Being the gem he is, he assists you by coming in early and doing some cardiac monitoring. True, he is a rare exception and not the rule; but honest communication was the key to success.

Now which appeals to you: direct patient care, teaching, or management?

Now that you have viewed several patient-care areas in which you might like to work, you need to know where to find each one. As mentioned in Chapter I, hospital restructuring has eliminated certain units from a given hospital, while emphasizing another. Some nursing-care situations are dealt with in special environments. Psychiatric hospitals are built to accommodate the mentally ill and are staffed with specially trained personnel. Before you narrow your field to one specialty, it is usually to your advantage to gain a minimum of one year's general experience, be it hospital or otherwise. Without that behind you, you lack the substance of patient care and the foundation to build on. The importance of your foundation cannot be overemphasized. It is on these first blocks that everything else is built. Promotions are likely to elude you without a solid foundation.

A likely first choice is an acute-care hospital. The next question is your geographical preference. Where would you feel most comfortable: in a large city, a small town, a rural setting, or a large teaching hospital? Study each setting before making your decision. There are tremendous differences.

A rural hospital is usually small, perhaps 100 beds, and houses all units in a very general way. The patient mixture is a little of everything. A drug overdose, a heart attack, and a head injury are all admitted to the Intensive Care Unit. By law, certain units must be separate entities (e.g., Pediatrics and Obstetrics). All surgicals, appendectomy to hysterectomy to gallbadder, would be self-contained on one unit, all medical cases on another wing. You may have patients with diabetes, an allergic reaction, and an uncomplicated back injury all on the same Medical Unit.

The critically ill or critically unstable patients are usually transferred as soon as possible, because small hospitals often lack the sophisticated resources available at metropolitan hospitals.

The employees of a small hospital are usually a cohesive team. Most nurses' meetings are informal and often spontaneous. Professional nursing changes are more slowly initiated and implemented. Seldom are "strangers" or "trainees" seen. The patients are friends, neighbors, your barber, or your banker. Visitors are usually well known. Student nurses and residents seldom train at rural hospitals, unless a medical university is nearby. Familiarity definitely affects your professional demeanor and your delivery of patient care. On the personal side, a rural town offers little to satisfy cultural needs or community activities.

At the other extreme is the large teaching research center, almost always associated with a four-year university. Such centers are usually situated in a large, culturally rich, and fast-paced city. The hospital itself is enormous. It is not uncommon to find a specialty division and several subdivisions all on one floor. There may be separate buildings, each representing a specialty hospital. To add to the confusion, there is often a Special Research Unit for patients with incurable diseases, a Rehabilitation Unit, a Head Injury–Trauma Unit, and a Hematologic Disorders Unit. The Emergency Room can be subdivided so that each diagnosis has a special admittance room. There may be Isolation Rooms used exclusively for isolation on each unit. A helicopter landing pad for transporting critically ill patients or donor organs may also be part of the scene.

University teaching hospitals present an overall higher level of continuous stress for the nurse. The nurse's work pattern is perpetual movement. The atmosphere, though not cold, is much more impersonal. Changes in routine can be abrupt and often radical. Patient-care conferences are frequent, and consequently more charting is required. The hospitals are technologically advanced, utilizing the most sophisticated monitoring equipment as soon as it becomes available.

Even though you may know the nurses on your floor, most large hospitals are decentralized; hospital-wide nurses' meetings are non-existent. Each unit has its nurses' meetings independent of others. Except during lunch or coffee break in the cafeteria, you probably would not meet nurses from different units. Patients are frequently from other cities or even other states. It is virtually impossible to become acquainted with everyone in a 1,000-bed hospital. To identify employees, each wears a picture ID.

These units are always bustling with health-care personnel, including medical students from a variety of disciplines. Physicians' orders can be changed three, four, or more times each shift because of patients' unstable conditions. Many new or radical procedures are performed as life-saving maneuvers in these hospitals before being practiced in smaller institutions. The patients on your unit all have the same kind of ailment. The interns, residents, and student nurses rotate so frequently that you do not have an opportunity to really know them. You and the nurses on your unit become the stabilizing force. The staff physicians make rounds with the residents, and the senior residents often write the doctors' orders, cosigned and authorized by the hospital staff physician. Staff physician and private physician are not synonymous. Although available, private physicians are not as prevalent. Most patients are assigned a bed according to their diagnosis, and the staff physician for that unit supervises their care.

Are you adaptable, flexible, and a quick thinker? Do you excel in interpersonal skills? Do you thrive on a fast pace? Do you enjoy the constant challenge of an ever-changing world around you? Are you independent and self-confident? Are you hungry for and able to grasp and apply new knowledge? Do technological advances excite you? Do you maintain a high energy level? If you answered yes to most of these questions, you would be ideal for the job.

Obviously, the descriptions of the rural hospital and the medical center are the extremes and have their exceptions, but the general highlights are universal. All other hospitals are sandwiched between the two extremes.

If you decide against hospital employment, there are numerous other options, including health maintenance organizations, numerous types of clinics, doctors' offices, home health agencies, and rehabilitation centers.

Do you like the consistency of working for one person, or a group of doctors, and learning their preferences? Do you like working with ambulatory patients? Do you enjoy knowing which procedures you will routinely perform? Do you like variety? Office and clinic nurses perform many procedures not usually done by hospital nurses. For example, nurses take X-rays in a doctor's office; in a hospital, an X-ray technician executes them. If the physician is a specialist, the nurse may be trained to perform advanced procedures.

Clinics that attend to specific diseases are easily recognized. Weight-loss clinics assist patients to lose weight under medical supervision. The nurse collaborates with the client and consults with the physician. Hypertension clinics help patients control their blood pressure on an outpatient basis. You would prepare a nursing-care plan and monitor the patient's progress. In mental health clinics, the nurse is a member of an interdisciplinary team that helps restore patients to mental health. In immunization clinics, nurses provide the public with inoculations to prevent illnesses.

There are a number of special purpose agencies that you could join. The Red Cross offers assistance here and abroad. This may be particularly attractive if you enjoy travel.

You may be a school nurse for children. The nurse's duties include checking health records, giving prescribed medications, assessing ill children, and performing routine checks for pests such as ringworm or head lice.

You may choose to work in a college setting as a nursing instructor, teaching others the intricacies of the profession.

Have you considered the armed forces? The Army Nurse Corps, Navy medical programs, the Marines and the Air Force offer an abundance of choices. The general requirement for the armed forces is graduation from a school of nursing accredited by the National League for Nursing. Preference is given to bachelor of science nurses; however, associate degree and diploma nurses are accepted with one or more years of hospital experience. Health requirements are fairly rigid. You are disqualified if you have any chronic anomaly, disease, or illness that inhibits normal functioning. If the armed forces interest you, see your local recruiter for details.

Conventional Nursing versus Nursing-Affiliated Positions? Conventional nursing is direct patient care in common nursing settings, as has been discussed. Nursing-affiliated positions include health consultants, technical writers, nurse practitioners, nurse clinicians, and accreditation surveyors.

As part of your nurse's training, you will have your clinical practicum in several places: hospitals, clinics, doctors' offices, schools, Public Health Departments, and nursing homes. After exposure to these, you will be better equipped to decide which you prefer. Volunteer or nurse's aide experience will give you valuable insight and a base to build on.

Research your area of choice so that your background is broad enough to provide an understanding of the field and to allow you to ask intelligent questions. Discussions with nurses can let you in on many lessons learned only through experience. There are countless things you do not learn from books because they are impossible to anticipate.

Observe other nurses in action so that you can get a feeling for the pace, the tension-stress level generated, the type of work, and other features that may influence your decision.

Hands-on experience is the ideal method of exploration. Your nurse's training will give you invaluable firsthand experience. If you have a choice of assignments, take the challenging unknown, not the familiar. Now is the time to collect the data that you will later process and apply to more complex situations. Your nursing assignments as a student should be diversified and plentiful. The sooner you gain experience, the better prepared you will be to make those all-important career decisions.

Conventional nursing revolves around direct patient care, and the common place is hospital units. However, there are variations in the types of positions available in such settings as hospitals and clinics. Some nurses work strictly in Infection Control. Nurse recruiters spend the majority of their time recruiting new staff. There are also unique nursing positions such as working on a cruise ship, as a camp nurse, or as an occupational health nurse. Working as a critical care transport nurse is terrific if you like to fly, travel, and render care to the critically ill.

Among nursing-affiliated positions, a nursing home administrator and health care administrator are easy to relate to because they are highly visible management positions. Each requires specialized training apart from nursing. Others are governing agencies, state accreditation bureaus, third-party reimbursement firms, and companies that ascertain that patient care meets standards. Common qualification minimums are an RN plus additional formal training tailored to the position. Medical sales representative is another alternative, especially for a nurse who enjoys both travel and sales. An excellent salary is a distinct possibility. Technical writing—reports, articles, books,

COURTESY KENLOCK CLINIC
An RN takes an X ray of a patient's wrist.

synopses, or any material pertaining to nursing and the health care field—is an alternative for a nurse who is adept at journalism.

Do You Seek Independent Functioning as an Employee or to Be Self-employed? Do you function best alone or as a team member? You function independently in hospital primary nursing care; however, other nurses are in close proximity as a support system and for consultation when desired. True independent functioning while in someone's employ occurs in private duty nursing. As a private duty nurse you are alone with the patient during your tour of duty, yet you are expected to collaborate with other health care professionals during patient-care conferences. True solitaire is not to be found in the world of nursing. Even those who own a business and function from their own office call their colleagues for advice and input. The longer you are isolated from other nurses, the further out of touch with reality you become. To stay abreast of technological advances, the changes in educational requirements, and the restructuring within the health care delivery system as they occur, you must stay in touch with other nurses in the nursing world.

A major drawback to working solitaire is that you can become a victim of burnout without recognizing the symptoms. The signs and symptoms are subtle, and sometimes it takes an outsider to see the changes. You live with yourself everyday and may fail to notice the unhealthy habits developing. Another possible complication is "isolationitis," or the loss of an immediate support system. It is imperative if you elect to work as an independent that you be an authority in your nursing area and that you guard against burnout and isolationitis.

If you really wish to be a nursing entrepreneur, the opportunities abound. You can be blocked only by your educational preparation, your clinical expertise, the laws controlling the profession, and your creativity, management skills, and business sense. Possible business ventures include consulting, being a nurse practitioner, and owning a medical supply store or home health care agency.

Once you have the basics and the framework, nursing is very pliable. Obtain a strong foundation, and then plan your future.

Some practicing nurses would never leave the patient's bedside. Some nurses who have their own business away from the patient's bedside incorporate direct patient care into their business format. For example, the owner of a medical-hospital supply shop assesses patients' needs, consults with physicians, communicates with families, and visits patients in their homes to ascertain that all is going well. Her nursing, management, and business sense will reap huge benefits in the future. Why will she be successful? She is applying both business and nursing skills to her career. She is helping clients and insurance companies save time and money by assisting patrons in making appropriate decisions and following doctors' orders. Physicians, other health personnel, and previous clients will refer newcomers to her. Word of mouth is the ideal means of marketing. It is targeted to those in need, at the precise moment of need, by those who know the facts about the company.

Chapter V

Finding a Nursing Position to Satisfy Your Needs

As a professional nurse, you have invested valuable time, money, and energy to achieve your status. It is of paramount importance for you to select your employment carefully in relation to your career needs. Your new position should foster your professional growth and maturation.

There are three primary job-finding methods for you to investigate: conventional, unconventional, and specialty.

Many nursing positions can be found using *conventional* methods. The yellow pages of the telephone book, newspaper classified advertisements, and referrals (commonly called networking) are three key sources of prospective employers. The quality of a referral should be scrupulously examined before you follow up.

Let us say you have two leads, both conveying the same message. Which of the two would you investigate, and why?

- Sue Bell, your neighbor, stops to talk with you at the mailbox. During the conversation, she tells you that Sheshon Hospital is recruiting Cardiac Care nurses on the afternoon shift.
- Carol Evans, a registered nurse employed by Sheshon Hospital, suggests that you call Mrs. Heron, Director of Nurses. If Mrs. Heron is not hiring Cardiac Care nurses, she may suggest a colleague who is.

You should have answered the second choice, and this is why:

- Carol Evans is an employee of the hospital and knows their needs better than an outsider.

- Carol has given you valuable information not always available. She has supplied you with the name of a contact, her title, and how to make the contact.
- Carol is a professional referral, or network. When researching job leads, it is advisable to follow professional suggestions when possible.

The advantages of conventional job-finding sources are ready availability and familiarity. The disadvantages are that they are confined to a given geographical location and that job offers in unique or specialty fields are often omitted.

Unconventional job-finding sources may open more doors to employment than the conventional means. Unfortunately, some people are unaware that they exist or do not realize their full potential. Before you read the want ads or dial the phone, you may want to explore some of these alternatives. Your county service department may have a health care services employment opportunities listing for your area. The government offers numerous permanent and contractual assignments in nursing and health care fields. The library can provide nursing employment reference books in which you can find new employment ideas. Some nursing schools offer health care placement services for both students and nonstudents. Valuable job information can be found in general nursing magazines. Important job-related facts are exchanged through general nursing associations open to all nurses and specialty organizations for nurses in particular fields of nursing. Any of these avenues may supply you with the knowledge required to find your ideal position.

The advantages of unconventional job-finding sources are essentially two: They broaden the possibilities offered by conventional means, and as a direct result they hold the potential for increased financial rewards.

Among the disadvantages, exhaustive research may be required to reveal a target prospective employer. A direct or indirect fee may be charged by some of these sources. Direct fees are charged for placement service by an organization. Indirect charges are incurred when you join a nursing organization and must pay membership dues.

Specialty job-finding sources are designed to help professional nurses locate a company that needs their particular expertise. Virtually every division of nursing has an exclusive association from which members can obtain statistics and idiosyncrasies regarding employment in its specialty. Supplemental specialty job-finding sources may include newsletters and placement agencies.

The primary advantages of specialty job-finding sources are unrestricted geographical listings and an abundance of inside information on employment possibilities in your specialty. These are very time-efficient. Your preliminary target market research has been done for you by a reliable source.

Among disadvantages, specialty job-finding sources are an asset only to a specialty nurse; the general staff nurse will derive only minimum benefits, if any. Also, travel expenses to conduct your pre-search might be prohibitive, or organization membership dues could be a deterrent.

Women jobseekers may want to investigate Wider Opportunities for Women, 1511 K Street, NW, Washington, DC 20005. Your county may have a Women's Resource Center to offer additional leads.

Select and organize your sources, and then build your job-seeking campaign. You should first assemble a Personalized Marketing Packet. To do so you must: make a comprehensive professional and personal assessment, organize your self-marketing campaign, and pre-search your prospective employer.

Step 1: Determine your professional and personal assessment guidelines.

- What are your professional goals?
- What discipline of nursing do you plan to pursue? Guesstimate your first, second, and third choices.
- Do you have geographical limitations? If so, be specific in listing them.
- How soon must you be gainfully employed? Translated, how long can you take to find the job you want?
- What type of setting appeals to you: rural, small town, large city?
- What is your preference of work environment? Your first choice might be a private clinic because you prefer ambulatory patient care and teaching. Your second choice could be a nursing home because you like geriatric nursing care. Your third choice might be a large acute-care teaching hospital because you thrive on challenge.
- Total your basic living expenses for one year, and then calculate your salary requirements to meet your cost of living. Try to

anticipate special expenses over the next year (you may need a new car) and add them to your list. Is your salary range still adequate?

- Identify your personal needs: Working midnights makes you physically ill; you must work afternoons because your continuing education classes are scheduled in the mornings.
- What personal attitudes, habits, standards, and philosophies would be major influencing factors in determining job prospects?

Step 2: Organize your self-marketing campaign. Define your target market. Then, using your job-finding sources, compile a list of ten to twenty candidates that are compatible with your professional and personal assessment.

Write a letter requesting literature from each institution. Their introductory brochures will probably outline special health care services offered and give you a basis for obtaining answers to other important questions.

Read each piece of literature critically and eliminate those that do not meet your personal criteria. Rank the prospective employers in order of compatibility. Transcribe the data from your professional assessment and the company's literature to your Choose Your Employer Card File. You might use a steno notebook, or 5″ by 7″ index cards, for a quick, one-stop reference check for all your employment information.

Choose Your Employer File Card
Personalized Marketing Packet Notes (PMPN)

Hospital	Rated #1
Location	Date
Contact Person and Title	
Phone #	
PMPN	
Nursing Specialty	
Pays for continuing education	
Meets geographical requirements	
Setting: rural	
Environment: private clinic	

Front of 5″ × 7″ Index Card

Presearch Data (recorded during your pre-search visit)	Method of Contact: (Phone, Mail, Personal)
Observations:	Date Initiated:
Communication:	Liked or Disliked:
Comments:	Comments:

Back of 5″ × 7″ Index Card

Next establish how you will approach your job-hunting project. Will you type your own cover letters and résumé or have them done by a word processor? What hours will you be available to answer your phone? Will someone answer your phone in your absence, or will you use a telephone-answering device to record messages? Remember, a missed phone call could mean a lost job opportunity.

Record all your expenses as they occur; they may be tax-deductible. Another thought, your prospective employer may give you complete or partial reimbursement. Keep an expense record for each prospective employer.

Expense Record

Expense record for _____ Hospital	
Travel (gas, food)	Clothes (if requirement of employment)
Phone (bill, answering service)	Miscellaneous
Job package (detailed explanation later)	

Step 3: Pre-search your prospective employer. This phase is critical to your success in obtaining the position best suited to your professional and personal convictions. A judicious performance will yield the exact job you want. A superficial scanning may result in unnecessary failure. Planning and evaluating are your tools to success.

Flip through your Choose Your Employer Card File; refresh your memory on your personalized marketing information and the literature received from the hospital or facility. Rank the ten to twenty viable prospects in order of preference. Your top five choices constitute your initial pre-search investigation. File, do not discard, the other prospects.

Before you start your intensive pre-search study, do a preliminary quick-scan to determine if a prospective employer is worth the time investment required. This is the fun part.

Your quick-scan consists of basic observations and analysis. Jump in your car or on the bus or subway and make a practice run to your prospective employer. In your excitement, do not forget your Choose Your Employer File Card for writing comments or taking out your aggressions, whichever is appropriate. Plan to travel during peak rush-hour traffic. Is this a relaxing trip, or are you aboard the white-knuckle express? One-way streets, traffic jams, and overcrowded trains all contribute to negative stress and can exhaust you before you begin your tour of duty. Are these small considerations? Maybe, but they could be the determining factor.

Once on location, capitalize on your observational skills. Is the visitors' parking lot well-kept or littered? Is there a parking attendant? Are the lawn and shrubs well manicured or neglected? Is the lobby clean and attractively furnished?

Why are these observations important? They give you an overview of the management's basic philosophies and the employees' attitudes and work habits. If these standards meet your approval, relax and continue your quick-scan. If the circumstances are unsatisfactory, waste no time; leave and continue to your next prospect. Make notes on your Choose Your Employer File Card of the conditions you found deplorable or your specific reasons for disapproval.

If the prospect is still a viable candidate, observe the visitors' and employees' behavioral transactions. Do staff and visitors interact with one another, or do they refrain from communicating? Specifically observe the employees. Do most of them send vibra-

Notice the well-kept building.

tions of contentment with pleasant facial expressions, or are most
of them sober, looking angry or depressed? Are negative or
positive reactions prevalent? As you make your subjective judgment, however, look carefully at the total picture. Everyone can
experience a bad day, and one incident (like the unexpected loss of
a patient) can have traumatic effects on all staff.

Now observe the employees' appearance. Are the majority neat
and clean, or wrinkled and dirty? Are you impressed with your
findings? If not, jot down major reasons for discontent and exit
promptly. If yes, make a few pertinent notes and plan for a return
pre-search trip. Record your travel time during rush hour, parking
costs for an employee, route directions to the site, and special facts
to remember. Before you leave, make detailed notes on visitors'
attire.

Do you still like what you see? As you continue your quick-scan,
check the employees' parking lot and notice the layout. Does the
lighting seem adequate for after dark? Is it close to the employee
exit door? It may be worthwhile to check safety features such as
security guards on duty or escorts available.

When you arrive home, while details are still fresh in your mind, plan your pre-search investigation for the next day, if possible. Plan your wardrobe and accessories, approximating the dress of the visitors on your quick-scan visit so that you will blend in and become one of the crowd. Your pre-search is not an advertised appearance. You are conducting an unobtrusive fact-finding mission to decide whether you would like to work there. Update your Choose Your Employer File Card in preparation for tomorrow.

For now, your pre-search arrival time has to be during the day, to permit you to flow with the visitors. Ideally, it should be during the shift you want to work. It is advisable to arrive half an hour before shift change, enabling you to encounter as many information-givers as possible. Observe and evaluate the staff as a unit, noticing attitudes, department affiliations, personal habits, and communication skills.

Upon arrival, walk to the main entrance of the building naturally, slowly, and deliberately. Absorb all the data your five senses provide. Your demeanor should be free, relaxed, and friendly. How do the employees react to you? Are the staff responsive to one another? Once in the lobby, head to the rest room and freshen up. As you leave the rest room, take the opportunity to observe the hospital atmosphere. Is it just busy, or very confused? Are hospital personnel helpful or aloof? Do most people seem happy or discontented? Is the general atmosphere flighty or organized, noisy or quiet? Next, study the floor layout. Which unit is on which floor? Where would you be working? Read and absorb all posted information. Are the visitors' rules rigid or flexible? Are they strictly adhered to or only quasi-enforced by the nurses? Who has been honored for contributions, and what kind? Have employees received awards for outstanding achievements or length of service? Or is attention focused on the unknown who made a large financial donation? Note the institution's priorities. Are patients' rights posted and taken seriously? What governing agencies accredit this company? What do you see: disorganization, uniformity, too stuffy, too large, too small, challenging, or boring? Are you impressed or depressed? If it does not meet your specifications, conserve your energy, make notes, and return home.

If you are interested, stick around! There is more to do. Activate your communication skills as you continue your pre-search investigation. Inconspicuously listen to the content and tone of conversations between employees and visitors and among employees. Do visitors seem pleased or disgusted with the care their loved one is receiving? Can you isolate a reason? Is one person being blamed? Is it an unjustified complaint indicating a personality conflict, or a justified complaint such as that the doctor poked him three times doing the spinal tap? Is an entire unit at fault? Maybe the Orthopedic Unit afternoon shift has consistently failed to give nighttime care to the same four patients. Isolate the cause of dissatisfaction. If several people voice the same negative opinion, you could consider the circumstances and investigate further. However, your wisest choice is probably to leave promptly and proceed with a new candidate; most internal problems are difficult to diagnose and resolve.

If circumstances still meet your specifications, try to find a friendly employee whom you can engage in conversation. Introduce yourself, explain the reason for your visit, say that you are impressed, and ask an open-ended question: Is this place as pleasant to work in as it seems? If you are fortunate, this person will be forthcoming. If not, do not press. Just say thank you and disappear. Then enter comments on your Choose Your Employer File Card, consider your visit a victory, and head home. You may find it advantageous to visit two or three times on the shift of your choice. There can be a remarkable difference in the personality types that work a given shift.

Repeat this process with each organization until you have collected all the facts you need to make an intelligent decision. Once you have narrowed your choices down to two or three, you are ready to write your professional nurse's job-winning package.

Professional Nurse's Job-winning Package

Write your résumé, cover letter, and other components slanted to the employer of your choice. The Four R's (rights) to remember are: mail your résumé and cover letter to the *right* person, containing the *right* message, in the *right* format, at the *right* time.

Referring to your Choose Your Employer File Card, address your mailing to the contact person stated. That is the *right* person. A contact person is missing? Check the job-finding source that provided this employer and the literature you received from the company. If you still lack a contact person, call the organization and ask for the name of the director of nursing. It is imperative that your material reach the Nursing Department.

The *right* message must be compatible with the company's philosophies and with your personal and professional assessment. Combine the philosophies you discovered in your pre-search investigation and your assessment of the company. Tell the employer how your skills complement their needs and expectations. The *right* format is the correct presentation of your résumé and cover letter.

The *right* time to apply for a position coincides with the employer's need to fill a position. Naturally, the optimum time to apply for work immediately precedes the need. This is where your professional networking is an invaluable assessment tool. Short of networking insights, check your pre-search survey. You may have picked up clues to internal factors that create specific needs. Student nurses frequently break for the summer and do not reconvene until fall term. Consider vacation shortages, especially summertime. During holidays and weekends, staffing is slashed to a minimum. It is fairly common to find the midnight and afternoon shifts short-staffed. You may want to consider contingency or call-in relief status, especially if part-time work is your preference. If you wish contingency status or afternoon and midnight shifts, be sure to mention it in your cover letter. It is a definite selling point. Keep in mind that the more flexible you are, the more in demand you will be.

You have completed the Four R's of your fact-finder's documentation. From this, you will compose your Job Package.

Your Job Package is a written fact sheet of your achievements, personality characteristics, career goals, natural abilities, and work-related habits. When presented as a complete unit, your written image becomes visible to the reader. The psychological, emotional, and mental you comes to life. Therefore, it is critical to your success that you choose and use action words that present you in the most favorable light.

What comprises your Job Package? Your résumé and cover letter that convey your central theme, your achievement record, your career goals, and your continuing education summary.

- State your *career goals* now and in the future, and possible strategies to meet those goals. Pull this from your reference sheets.

- Use your *superior achievements sheet* to briefly describe an exceptional accomplishment, such as having resolved or made a major contribution to the resolution of a Nursing Department problem.

- Your *continuing education sheet* lists the courses you have taken that exceed minimum nursing requirements. It can also mention nursing school or extracurricular community activities you have engaged in that facilitated health care–oriented learning. Nursing journals or books you have read on your own may or may not be granted official credit.

- List any *professional affiliation* such as membership in professional organizations, clubs, and associations that foster professional growth.

- Your *cover letter* offers your prospective employer the first glimpse of your written image. If compatibility has been established with the employer and you have properly handled your cover letter, your candidacy will probably be considered. If improperly handled, even though you have the qualifications you could lose all chance of getting the job you want.

- Your *résumé* should tell the employer where you have worked and your accomplishments during your tenure. If you are a nursing student or a recent graduate, you should give your school and your anticipated date of graduation as well as noteworthy academic or clinical accomplishments.

- A *cover letter–résumé* is a condensed and combined version of the cover letter and résumé. It is ideally used by one with a fragile employment history, or by new graduates.

- Your *letters of reference* are evidence of your achievements and attributes. Each is a valuable testimony to your excellence. Who is qualified to write your letters of reference? Previous employers, nursing instructors, or health care professionals. Character references can be from anyone who is not a relative, preferably a health care professional or respected community leader. To assure yourself of getting a letter of reference from the person of your choice, you should request it before your work relationship terminates and your status becomes history. After graduation, an instructor may forget some of your outstanding features. A letter of reference is written by someone who admires you and wants to help you achieve your career and personal aspirations. Do not misuse letters of reference. Always request permission from the writers before submitting their letters. If possible, inform them who might be calling or writing, and when.

If you have not already determined your *career goals*, do so now.

Step 1: List two to three goals you would like to achieve during the next twelve months.

* To be a Cardiac Care staff nurse.
* To be a psychiatric nurse in a private ambulatory clinic.
* To be an inservice director in a rural setting.

Step 2: Rank your goals in order of importance.

Step 3: Research each goal to determine for which you have the educational and technical training and which would need additional training and education to pursue. Elementary prerequisites for these positions are as follows:

* The Cardiac Care staff nurse position requires specialty theory classes and corresponding clinical practicum. This training usually takes three months.
* There are no specific prerequisites to be a psychiatric nurse in a private ambulatory mental health clinic; however, most suggest extra classes or additional in-house inservices.
* Inservice director requires formal education, usually consisting of a bachelor's or advanced degree and some staff nurse experience.

Step 4: Eliminate those that do not meet your one-year time frame: in this example, inservice director in a rural setting.

Step 5: Number the remaining goals in order of importance and immediate attainability.

* To be a Cardiac Care staff nurse.
* To be a psychiatric nurse in a private ambulatory clinic.

Step 6: Write the final copy of your career goals.

To secure employment as a Cardiac Care staff nurse, where my specialized skills and advanced education will be used to mutual benefit, providing financial rewards compatible with my responsibilities, and offering possibilities of advancement.

To secure employment as a psychiatric nurse in an ambulatory environment conducive to professional growth, by fostering continuing education in mental health using my specialized training and skills to mutual advantage, and offering financial recompense and promotional possibilities.

Step 7: Proofread for grammar, punctuation, and sentence structure, and then retype if necessary.

Your *superior achievements sheet* tells your prospective employer about something unique or profound you have accomplished, or about a professional nursing talent you possess. The final copy of your superior achievements sheet may read like this: You prepared and delivered a 1-1/2-hour workshop on stress as a nursing theory class requirement. Lecture contents emphasized recognizing when positive stress becomes negative and appropriate coping mechanisms. Role playing was employed by the nurse as common Cardiac Care Unit problems were identified, resolved, and evaluated. Coping mechanisms were classified by the behavioral transaction that occurred as an interaction, an action, or a reaction.

Your *continuing education sheet* includes all learning experiences that enhance your nursing expertise or broaden your knowledge base.

Continuing education is defined as a lifelong learning process. It can mean formal education, for which you receive college credit; or informal learning, which can be inservices, workshops, or seminars.

Step 1: Record all your continuing education during the last five years.

- "Should You Be a Cardiac Care Nurse"
  Nursing Specialty Jan/Feb '88 (magazine)
  2/88 .4 CEU

- Holistic Patient Assessment–2 credits
  Basic Cardiac Rhythms and Arrhythmias–4 credits
  Bright University
  Bright, Maine 49137
  1/88-4/88

Step 2: If you have more than one page, eliminate the oldest or least significant first, with magazine articles being least significant. If you are a new graduate, highlight all extra nursing-related projects in which you have been involved.

Step 3: Place your continuing education in chronological order, with the most recent first. If you have only a few as a new graduate, place the emphasis on the most significant.

Step 4: Double-check for accuracy, grammar, and consistency, and type a perfect sheet.

The final copy of your continuing education sheet:

- Basic Cardiac Rhythms and Arrhythmias–4 credits
  Bright University
  Bright,Maine 49137
  1/88–4/88

- Holistic Patient Assessment–2 credits

- "Should You Be a Cardiac Care Nurse"
  Nursing Specialty   Jan/Feb '88   (magazine)
  2/88   .4 CEU

Your *professional affiliations* should be listed on a separate sheet of paper. (If you have not joined a student nurses' association or nurses' association, you may want to investigate the possibility. They may answer many of your questions, offer networking, and give you a head start.)

Your *cover letter* should help the prospective employer decide whether to take time to read your résumé. It reveals such traits as self-confidence, ability to communicate, accuracy when recording facts, stability, and integrity. If you are logical, organized, and neat, the depth of your people skills will also be revealed. It is amazing what a few sentences can tell an insightful reader. *Note:* A cover letter is *one page maximum*; state your facts clearly and concisely.

- Contents and flow of your cover letter should state your reason for writing.
- Introduce the prospective employer to your résumé and job package.
- Let your qualifications state why you are the ideal candidate for the position. (Be certain to specify the position; the organization may have more than one vacancy to fill.)

- Highlight your special achievements and ways you could benefit this particular company.
- Briefly mention your primary career goal.
- State your interview follow-up plan.

The final copy of your cover letter:

> Jackie Johnson
> 6161 Rose Lake Drive
> Oakville, Michigan 46016
> 1-804-622-1905

Sheshon Community Clinic
505 East Hartford
Sheshon, Michigan 44001

Attention Mrs. Ashbay, RN, Director of Nursing

Dear Mrs. Ashbay:

In response to your advertisement in the Oakville *County Press*, I am enclosing my résumé. I am interested in a Cardiac Care staff nurse position.

I am a recent graduate of Maple University, and will take my state boards in about six weeks.

I have completed all the mandatory Cardiac Care classes. I possess excellent patient assessment skills, and I am adept at interpersonal skills. I cope effectively with emergencies and with the prolonged periods of high stress that mark the atmosphere of most Cardiac Care Units.

I have prepared and presented a 1-1/2 hour workshop on "Recognizing When Positive Stress Becomes Negative, and Appropriate Coping Mechanisms." I would be delighted to do a mini-demonstration to show you how this could complement your unit.

My immediate goal is to establish rapport with co-workers and others. With the assistance of my head nurse, I would like to structure a clinical-technical program that will qualify me for administrative advancement and certification as a Cardiac Care nurse.

I will be available for an interview from February 10 through 21. Acknowledgment of receipt of the enclosed résumé would be greatly appreciated. For your convenience, a self-addressed stamped envelope has been provided for that purpose. Thank you for your time and consideration.

Respectfully,

Jackie Johnson

The contents of your résumé or cover letter–résumé would be arrived at the same way.

Step 1: If you are a student nurse or a recent graduate without an impressive employment record, take two sheets of paper and mark one *theory* and the other *clinical*.

Theory	Clinical

Step 2: List your achievements in each area that are consistent with your career goals.

Theory

Studied and performed intensive investigations of psychological reactions to heart attacks; wrote summary report.

Wrote and presented a 1-1/2 hour workshop on stress and appropriate coping mechanisms.

Clinical

Acquired skills to give accurate and complete cardio-vascular assessment.

Devised and perfected patient teaching program for rehabilitative cardiac patients.

Step 3: Rank your achievements in order of importance to you.

Theory

Studied and performed intensive investigations of psychological reactions to heart attacks; wrote summary report.

Wrote and presented a 1-1/2 hour workshop on stress and appropriate coping mechanisms.

Clinical

Devised and perfected patient teaching program for rehabilitative cardiac patients.

Acquired skills to give accurate and complete cardio-vascular assessment.

Step 4: Set up two columns headed *Skills* and *Achievements.* Transfer all your achievements to this sheet.

Skills	Achievements
	Investigated and reported psychological reactions to heart attacks. Wrote and presented a workshop on stress. Devised a rehabilitative cardiac teaching program. Performed cardiovascular assessment.

Step 5: Identify the skills that made your achievements possible.

Skills	Achievements
Communication Motivation Organization Self-starter Use of resources Prioritizing Retain and apply learned data Interpersonal skills	Investigated and reported psychological reactions to heart attacks. Wrote and presented a workshop on stress. Devised a rehabilitative cardiac teaching program. Performed cardiovascular assessment.

Step 6: Number the skills and match them to the corresponding achievements. It may require several skills to make one achievement.

Skills	Achievements	Match
1-Communication 2-Motivation 3-Organization 4-Self-starter	Investigated and reported psychological reactions to heart attacks.	1,2, 3,4

Step 7: Make a résumé Content Chart. List your achievements and analyze each completely. This is not a difficult exercise. However, some people omit important sections because they do not see how what they do can have such a tremendous impact on their environment and other people. Think *self-worth* as you complete this section.

Résumé Content Chart

1	2	3	4	5
Achievement	*Who Was Affected*	*Results*	*Skills Required*	*Who Commended Your Contribution*
1) Stress Workshop	Nursing personnel	Reduced negative stress	Communication Motivation Organization Self-starter	Nursing administration

Now that you have collected all the information required to write your résumé, here are a few common-sense rules. Résumés are best kept to one page, but two pages is the absolute maximum. Most employers do not have time to read page after page; besides, too much information distracts from your outstanding qualities.

As shown in the following paragraph, the body of your résumé will be derived from your Résumé Content Chart, which you have just completed.

Prepared and conducted stress workshops to increase nursing personnel's awareness of stress levels, differentiating negative and positive stress, while implementing effective coping mechanisms. As a result self-confidence was increased, reducing and controlling negative stress levels and creating an environment conducive to quality patient care.

Now construct the final copy of your résumé.

Career Goal:
To secure employment as a Cardiac Care nurse where my specialized skills and advanced education will be used to mutual benefit, providing financial rewards compatible with responsibilities, and offering advancement possibilities.

School of Nursing:
Maple University
Maple Leaf, Michigan 44863

Brief Job Description:
Graduated 4/28/88 from Bachelor of Science program with a 3.2 grade point average.

Major Accomplishments:
Prepared and conducted stress workshops to increase nursing personnel's awareness of stress levels, differentiating negative and positive stress, while implementing effective coping mechanisms. As a result self-confidence was increased, reducing and controlling negative stress levels and creating an environment conducive to quality patient care.

Acquired skills to give accurate patient assessment of physical (emphasizing cardiovascular), emotional, psychological, and mental needs. Formulated and activated a patient care plan to meet patients' changing needs.

Continuing Education Credentials:
Basic Cardiac Rhythms and Arrhythmias–4 credits
Bright University
Bright, Maine 49137
1/88–4.88
Holistic Patient Assessment–2 credits
"Should You Be a Cardiac Care Nurse"
Nursing Specialty Jan/Feb '88 (magazine)
2/88   .4 CEU

Professional Affiliations:
Active Student Nurses' Association
111 Blankview
Everville, Illinois 60011

Professional Nurses' Organization
77 Lewis Drive
Onesville, California 93354

Other Data:
Salary open to negotiation.
References available upon request.

If you elect to do a cover letter–résumé, heed these suggestions.

Step 1: Commence by stating your reason for writing.
Step 2: List your qualifications, stating why you are the ideal candidate for the position.
Step 3: Highlight your special achievements and ways you could benefit your target company.
Step 4: State your primary career goal, and conclude by stating your interview follow-up plan.

Following are suggested contents of a letter of reference written by another for you.

- If written by an employer, it should give dates of employment. If written by an instructor, a counselor, a community leader, a pastor, or a coach, give the length of acquaintanceship.
- Outline your major accomplishments that the writer has noted.
- State your health and attendance record.
- Comment on your personal attitude and outstanding personality traits.

Usually three letters of reference are all you need. Many prospective employers send a reference check form to be filled out, or simply make a phone call.

> Maple University
> School of Nursing
> 881 Main Street
> Mapleleaf, Michigan 48863

Sheshon Community Clinic
505 East Hartford
Sheshon, Michigan 44001

> Attention Mrs. Ashbay, RN, Director of Nursing

Dear Mrs. Ashbay:

Jackie Johnson graduated from our nursing program in April, 1988, with honors and a grade point average of 3.2. During the last two years, I have had ample opportunity to evaluate Jackie's performance in clinical and theory.

Jackie has many attributes that contribute to her excellence as a nurse, but I have been quite impressed with her interpersonal skills. She has perfected her oral and nonverbal communication, establishes easy rapport with patients, visitors, subordinates, colleagues, and superiors, and contributes to a cohesive team.

Jackie is prompt, punctual, and reliable, without excessive absenteeism. She is afflicted with a medical handicap, but it is not reflected in her performance or attendance record.

Jackie is conscientious and vivacious, showing a tremendous love for her profession. She exceeds requirements on all clinical and written assignments, with meticulous attention to detail. She is acutely responsive to her ethical, moral, and legal responsibilities. Her patient assessment skills are accurate and comprehensive.

It is with great pleasure that I recommend Jackie, a superior all-around student. She would be an asset to your Cardiac Care Unit and an excellent prospect for an administrative position. If I may provide additional information, your inquiry will be welcomed.

Respectfully,

Mrs. Evelyn Edwards

It is business etiquette to mail your completed job package in a legal-size envelope of the same color and stock as your paper.

Jackie Johnson
6161 Rose Lake Drive
Oakville, Michigan 46016

Sheshon Community Clinic
505 East Hartford
Sheshon, Michigan 44001

Att: Mrs. Ashbay, RN, DON

CONFIDENTIAL

Review your project in its entirety. Does it tell the prospective employer that you are the ideal candidate for the position? If so, type each page meticulously and head to the print shop. If you are on a limited budget, ask the print shop to help you choose good-quality bond paper in a subtle business color. Please, no bright vibrant colors. Then ask the print shop to run copies on the press. You will probably pay more than for an ordinary copy machine, but the quality will be superior and more cost-efficient than typesetting. Just be certain that the typing, paper stock, and color are identical.

Understanding the Employee Selection Process

Before the prospective employer ever reads your résumé and cover letter, he or she has a definite need to fill and has determined what qualifications and personality type will best meet those needs. The purpose of the selection process is to determine which applicant makes a match.

The prospective employer will evaluate your résumé and cover letter. If you are called in for an interview, Phase 1 is complete. The director of nursing will continue the selection process in Phase 2, the interview. Phase 3, your probationary period, is the final phase of the selection process.

Phase 1 of the selection process begins as the prospective employer glances at your envelope. Did you accurately type all the information? Did you include your return address? Is the contact person's name spelled correctly, and title included? Is the color of the envelope appropriate? As the prospective employer removes the contents from the envelope, does the paper match the envelope? Do all the pages match? Are they neatly or haphazardly folded? Let us stop for a moment. What could the reader surmise? Not much, you say? Wrong! The envelope can reveal whether you are neat, detail-oriented, accurate, and respectful of authority.

Phase 1 continues as the employer reads your cover letter. He could surmise that you are energetic, since you are seeking employment while preparing for state boards. Your grade point must be 3.0 or higher for you to qualify to take the supplemental cardiac training. Your people skills indicate that you are probably a good communicator. Your letter is well organized, and your priorities have been established. You are progressive and results-oriented. You are courteous and self-confident with your self-addressed stamped envelope and your interview follow-up instructions, respectively. Within a minute the employer has decided to read your résumé or place you in the "no thanks" file. If your résumé portrays the same favorable traits, you may receive a letter or phone call with an invitation to an interview.

Your prospective employer will be prepared to ask you questions about your expertise to assess your suitability for the position. By reviewing your Job Package, you can deduce many of the likely questions. This should be the first step in your pre-interview preparation.

Your pre-interview preparation should begin with a thorough mental, physical, psychological, and emotional assessment of your written package. What did you say in your cover letter and résumé? What questions might be asked about the contents of the enclosures? Remember, the director's goal is to staff the Cardiac Care Unit with a team of qualified nurses to meet hospital, patient, and accreditation bureau standards.

Since you are preparing for state boards, is accepting your first full-time staff nurse position in a specialty unit going to be too stressful? Be prepared to tell your interviewer which of your qualities and skills will enable you to handle the stress and your specific plans for coping with it. Information confirming the appointed date of your state boards would be helpful, and do not omit your nursing permit. Refresh your memory, and if possible take with you the class syllabus detailing the content of the supplemental Cardiac Care course. Will you need time off to study for and take the state boards? These arrangements should be agreed upon in advance. Be clear about your needs. If the company will not compromise to meet those needs before hiring, it could be a warning that your needs would be forgotten after employment. You have emphasized your superior interpersonal skills. You may be asked hypothetical questions such as "What would you do with this personality conflict?" You may be asked to give a clinical demonstration of your patient assessment skills. Since you have stated that you cope effectively with a variety of emergencies, you could be asked how you would respond to a given emergency. You have offered to perform a stress workshop, and you may be given the opportunity.

As you prepare for your interview, keep in mind that your future supervisor has many aspects to consider beyond the obvious. Budgetary allowance is a major consideration. Will you be the most cost-effective, as well as efficient, employee? Will your absenteeism rate be above average? Be ready to assure your prospective superior that your track record is good. Will you be the candidate to meet the Cardiac Care Unit's needs with the least additional training? Stress your supplemental Cardiac Care classes. Retention of personnel and length of service of employees play major roles in choice of future employees. Emphasize your loyalty to the facility in exchange for its nurturing your professional goals.

During the interview, your physical appearance and conduct will be evaluated, as well as your nursing aptitude. Perfect your physical image by paying particular attention to your grooming, attire, general health, and rest. Areas of conduct and behavior to receive special attention include mental status, attitude, alertness, and knowledge of the subject being discussed. The emotional state to project is one of calm, appropriate responses, and self-confidence. The psychological state of mind should display active communication, particularly nonverbal, and socially acceptable coping mechanisms. A very important factor to your success is to know yourself. You can then answer any question asked about your interactions, reactions, and actions, your stress level, others' perception of you, and your perception of others. No one can advise you how to respond to specific questions, but knowing yourself and responding honestly is your best insurance of finding the ideal position. You are not obligated to take the first or any job offer.

Collect your Choose Your Employer File Card, your complete Job Package, and information you have compiled from your résumé and cover letter review. Compile a list of questions you could ask at the interview that would promote your understanding of hospital philosophies and working conditions critical to your final decision. What is the total patient capacity and average census? What is the nurse-patient ratio on afternoons, weekdays, and weekends? What is the average age of your cardiac patients, the common diagnosis, and the general unit setup? Are Emergency Room medications obtained from the pharmacy or stock floor medications? Is there a physician on the premises at all times? If not, what is the on-call response time? Decide in advance what you consider good, tolerable, and intolerable working conditions. Plan your response to intolerable situations without being abrasive or dictatorial.

The interview process is not difficult if you are prepared. Thanks to your pre-search, you know your destination, the best route to take, travel time, and how to find the director's office.

You should dress in tastefully conservative business attire. Men should wear a suit. Save the female-catching aftershave for another day. Pay special attention to your grooming. For women a skirt and blazer or a dress with matching jacket or blazer is appropriate. No jewelry or makeup that screams "look at me." Pants suits are not acceptable. Grooming is important, with no overpowering perfume.

When you arrive at the facility, allow yourself a few minutes to review all your written documentation. From the second you enter the building be acutely aware of your personal presentment. Once in the lobby, go to the rest room and make one last head-to-toe inspection of your appearance. At the door of the director's office, remember that every move or comment you make can count. Think about your posture, handshake, eye contact, gestures, and nervous habits. You can bet your future that the director will. The moment of truth has arrived.

A special note: Dress for your chosen position. A director of nursing services sent an applicant to laundry services because she was dressed in blue jeans. An applicant assured the director that she handled emergencies admirably, yet sat biting her lip and fumbling with papers. What do you think?

As you wait in the director's office, quietly read a nursing-oriented or neutral magazine. When invited into the office, offer a handshake, introduce yourself, and wait for an invitation to be seated. The tone of the interview can be set by the handshake, introduction, and seating. Was the introduction formal or informal? Was the seating arrangement openly friendly and approachable, or aloof and authoritarian? Was the handshake assertive, passive, or aggressive?

The format of a typical nursing interview is a straightforward question and answer exchange. Chances are it will open with confirmation of the information you presented in your cover letter and résumé. Before the close of the interview, you will probably be offered the opportunity to ask questions that have not been answered. If not, by all means ask! You can effectively close the interview by asking the interviewer if you are a viable candidate. Be prepared for a rejection if you choose this closing, but usually this is the transition into your interview follow-up discussion. A tour of the facility gives you yet another opportunity to let your five senses work for you, and can be an indication that you are indeed a viable candidate.

As a rule, directors are a close-knit group of professionals. If a director thinks the information you have presented may be inaccurate, or that you may be a problem child, or that you sound too good to be true, he or she will probably check with a few colleagues. Directors maintain networks of colleagues on whom they rely. There is no easy escape if you earn a poor reputation. If you have major problems, your only chance for survival is to admit them and work to change each one. If you are not at fault for an incident, honestly explain your point of view.

An interviewer's questions are specifically relevant to the staff nurse position you seek. Incidentally, most states have guidelines on questions an employer can and cannot legally ask. Contact the Department of Civil Rights in your state for a copy of *Pre-Employment Inquiry Guide*.

What were the contents of the supplemental Cardiac Care classes you attended? When did you attend? What was the length of the program? Which college presented this program? How many hours of supervised clinical practicum did you experience? What preparations are yet to be made for your state boards? Do you need time off to study? Will you need time off to take your exam? What is your attendance record? How much and what patient teaching have you done?

How soon do you hope to progress to an administrative position? What additional management and clinical preparation do you think you will need? Can you analyze problems effectively, and are you capable of initiating a solution? Give me an example, (Your communication skills will be silently assessed without your knowledge.)

You say you cope with emergencies effectively. What procedure would you follow if a patient or visitor threatened you, or another, with a gun or knife?

Why have you chosen our institution as a place of employment? (If you pre-searched your prospective employer, you will be able to answer intelligently.) Precisely what can you do for this company? (Insert your skills, and state your career goals upon hiring.) Will you be able to handle the position? Do you possess the skills, knowledge, and experience to carry the job? If hired, will you be punctual? Will you put in a productive day's work? How long will you stay satisfactorily employed at this facility? How long do you estimate it will take you to master the job and become profitable to the organization? Will you work well with your colleagues and the interviewer? Do you possess a problem-creating personality flaw? Would you cause discredit to your supervisor, thus preventing raise or promotion? Are you a self-starter, or do you need to be cranked?

As you answer the questions, the director will compare your responses to those of the other applicants and may be drawing conclusions during the interview process.

As you terminate the interview, keep in mind that even if you are not hired, there may be good reasons. It could be to your advantage. The director of nurses is an expert at putting a team together, and your personality may not be compatible. Or your professional growth could be stifled, or the hospital philosophies are in direct conflict with yours. Your skills may be substandard for this particular unit's requirements; consider the consequences to your professional and personal integrity if your skills were not comparable to staff of the same classification. Before you feel rejected, or that the interview was a waste, look objectively at all the facts.

Whether the interview was negative or positive, thank your prospective employer before you leave. Once outside, make notes on your Choose Your Employer File Card and prepare to write your postinterview follow-up.

At home, write a thank-you note for the interview before you forget. The thank-you note should state the purpose of the note and the issues and points discussed during the interview. You should confirm your understanding of the prospective employer's comments. Thank the receptionist and others you met for their hospitality, and say a kind word or two about the institution. Finally, add to or correct impressions left behind.

Postinterview Follow-up Note

Jackie Johnson
6161 Rose Lake Drive
Oakville, Michigan 46016
1-804-622-1905

Sheshon Community Clinic
505 East Hartford
Sheshon, Michigan 44001

Dear Mrs. Ashbay:

I am interested in the second-shift Cardiac Care staff nurse
position I interviewed for on February 12, 1988, and would truly
appreciate your consideration.

I am enclosing for you to review at your convenience my
supplemental Cardiac Care Class Syllabus and corresponding
transcripts. As you recommended, I contacted Mrs. Steuber, and
I am scheduled to present my Stress Workshop on February 19 at
3:00 p.m. for this month's inservice. Sue Edwards, the CCU
head nurse, confirmed that upon my hiring she would assist me
in structuring my clinical-technical program to help me reach my
goal of administrative advancement.

You said that I would be given the week of state boards off.
You also advised me that an inservice orientation program would
be provided to allow a solid transition to the unit.

A special thank-you to Kay Evans, your receptionist, for her
kind assistance and offering refreshments. Your time,
explanations, and consideration are greatly appreciated. I look
forward to working with you in the near future.

Respectfully,

Jackie Johnson

Structure Your Position to Meet Your Future Expectations

For a position to be serviceable, it must meet your present needs and mold to meet your ever-changing objectives. Begin by accepting or declining a position you have just been offered.

Two weeks after your interview at Sheshon Hospital, the director of nursing calls to offer you the CCU staff nurse position you applied for. In the interim you had continued to interview, and as a result you have been offered an ideal balance of clinical experience and theory at the Northwestern Cardiac Rehabilitation and Catheterization Clinic. You have a dilemma. Which position will you take? How will you accept one and reject the other? Refer to your Choose Your Employer File Card and evaluate both offers. When you have completed your review, you decide the clinic is best suited to your needs. What will you do about the hospital?

- Call and say no thanks, explaining that you have been offered a position tailored to your needs.
- Ignore the hospital.
- Send a letter of explanation, declining the position.

Ignoring the hospital is both inappropriate and inconsiderate, and therefore not an option. You may wish to seek employment there another time.

Would a letter or phone call be the most appropriate means of declining the offer? If the interview was formal, only a written declination is proper. If the interview was informal and your phone inquiries have been welcomed, a phone conversation would be appropriate. However, phone conversations quickly become ancient history, and you become a forgotten entity. Letters are not soon forgotten. If you do opt to call first, back it with a written explanation.

A letter declining a position should be direct, brief, honest, considerate, and logical. Include your reason for writing, the position you were offered, and your thanks.

Jackie Johnson
6161 Rose Lake Drive
Oakville, Michigan 46016
1-804-622-1905

Sheshon Community Clinic
505 East Hartford
Sheshon, Michigan 44001

Dear Mrs. Ashbay:

I am writing to thank you for offering me a Cardiac Care staff nurse position on your second shift. Since our last meeting, however, I have been offered a position more compatible with my career goal of securing direct training for my Cardiac Care certification.

Your time, consideration, and offer are greatly appreciated. Possibly I could be of service to you another time.

I will still present my Stress Workshop on February 19 and would be delighted if you could attend.

Yours sincerely,

Jackie Johnson

Your logical evaluation is probably quite comprehensible to most nursing administrators. Chances are excellent that the director will attend the workshop and make notes to be attached to your application file.

The same rules apply in sending a letter of acceptance or making the confirmation by phone. A short letter solidifies your acceptance and prevents any misunderstandings.

Jackie Johnson
6161 Rose Lake Drive
Oakville, Michigan 46016
1-804-622-1905

Sue McIvory, Director of Services
Northwestern Cardiac Clinic
333 Northwestern Highway
Northwestern, Michigan 44601

Dear Ms. McIvory:

I am writing to confirm my appointment to the position of Cardiac Care nurse on your acute therapy unit.

I will report for my physical on March 1, 1988, and my tour of duty orientation on March 8. Incidentally, Carrie scheduled my open registration Stress Workshop for March 12 at 2:15 p.m.

Thank you for your time, and I look forward to working with you very soon.

Sincerely,

Jackie Johnson

How will you handle your probationary/orientation period? When you are newly hired, you are usually given an orientation period to familiarize yourself with the intricacies of the company, and you are sometimes considered on probation for a period of time. Individual company policy dictates the time frame, but it is commonly three months. During this period, your immediate supervisor observes and evaluates you on the job. All aspects of your performance, from your technical skills to your attitude, are taken into consideration before it is decided whether you will be retained as a permanent employee or dismissed because of an unresolvable problem. This is the last major checkpoint before the launch into permanent ties. While your employer is evaluating you, you should be examining your employer. Take advantage of your golden time of assessment.

- Learn the systems of the facility.
- Ask any questions that occur to you.

- Establish and perfect your daily routines.
- Present your facts to your superior. Make a special effort to address any problems you may have encountered. This is the time to solve them, or at least confront them honestly.
- Assess your skills in relation to your position and to colleagues performing identical functions.
- Implement steps to improve your weak points.
- Make plans for your advancement at this employer.
- Form your communication network of superiors, colleagues, and subordinates.
- Weigh the benefits against the disadvantages of the position.
- Make a smooth transition to permanent employment, or professionally make your departure.

Just as an employer has the right to release you without obligation during the probationary period, you have the right to resign without using the employer as a reference. After the probationary period, however, your status is changed to permanent and the situation changes drastically, from a simple note to a complex process. If you have decided this is not what you want, resign amicably.

You have been employed for six months, the afternoon charge nurse position will be vacant in two months, and you want a promotion. Critically evaluate your status to determine if you are qualified for and really want the position. If possible, talk with the present charge nurse and other charge nurses to find out what hidden responsibilities they may have. Strip the glory, and then decide if you want the extra hours and headaches that come with the job. What financial rewards will you receive for the advancement? What changes do you foresee in your schedule, team members, superiors, and environment? Will you be responsible for any new machines? Will you be in a new location?

Check out all the details. If they please you, follow your employer's promotion procedures to the last detail. Complete and submit forms to the proper person. When you apply for the promotion, dress and act accordingly. Pay special attention to your grooming, etiquette, and conduct. Be careful not to be too social. Business is business, and familiarity can backfire.

Let's say you were denied the promotion, and you feel you would be better appreciated elsewhere. If you are quitting, leave the door open behind you. You never know when that open door may be a welcome sight under new circumstances. Even if the conditions do not meet your standards, do not leave angry; just leave. Your termination should remain friendly and in accord with good business ethics.

Know when it is time for you to move on. Has your professional expertise been stifled or stunted? Are you a victim of burnout? Shame on you! Get in touch with yourself! As you prepare to resign, write a letter of resignation to your immediate supervisor, briefly explaining why you are departing and when. Above all, express thanks for the opportunity of having been an employee. Submit it as soon as feasible. That allows preparations to be made to replace you, while maintaining cohesion of the unit and facilitating a smooth transition.

Jackie Johnson
6161 Rose Lake Drive
Oakville, Michigan 46016

Sue McIvory, Director of Services
Northwestern Cardiac Clinic
333 Northwestern Highway
Northwestern, Michigan 44601

Dear Ms. McIvory:

I regretfully submit my resignation on this date, March 10, 1988, effective March 24, 1988.

I plan to begin my certification advanced cardiac studies on March 31.

During my tenure, I have gained bountiful knowledge in catheterizations and rehabilitative cardiac teaching. I wish to thank you for your assistance toward attaining my ultimate goal.

The employees I have worked with are terrific, and I will miss everyone. Good luck in your future endeavors.

Sincerely yours,

Jackie Johnson

Request an exit interview with your superior, the Personnel Department, the Chief of Staff, or any authority to whom you can give an honest appraisal. You will want to review your personnel file, to discuss why you are leaving as honestly as possible, and to offer suggestions for changes that would create a more positive work atmosphere. Some badly needed changes may not be mentioned by employees for fear of job loss. You are free to say what you want within reason. Use the opportunity to say goodbye and express your appreciation. This is the time to request references.

An exit interview differs sharply from an entrance interview. Its purpose is to close any communication gaps and terminate a business relationship. Conduct during an exit interview can be informal and led by either you or the employer.

Before you walk out the door for the last time as an employee, complete all ongoing projects. Tie the loose ends so that the next nurse can pick up where you left off. Offer to orient your replacement. Give the next nurse the added edge that will make the job easier. Help everyone to achieve a smooth transition. Put in a full day's work on your last day! You owe it to yourself for everyone's memories of you to be pleasant.

Rate your Compatibility with Nursing

As you have read this book, you have subconsciously drawn some conclusions. What were your intellectual-emotional reactions to the illustrations presented? If most situations elicited positive reactions, compatibility seems inevitable. On the contrary, if most of the situations left you perplexed, depressed, confused, or generally dissatisfied, you may not be a viable nursing candidate. Think carefully, then follow your intuition. Nursing is a rich profession with very special rewards, but there is a price to pay. Good luck with your decision.

Reader's Checklist

Name three types of job-finding sources? conventional, unconventional, and specialized.

What constitutes your Personalized Marketing Packet? Your professional and personal assessment.

Why would you pre-search a prospective employer? To help decide, before an interview, whether or not you would like to work there.

Match the items in the two columns.

Career goals	Extracurricular health care learning
Superior achievements	First glimpse of written image
Continuing Education	Alternate to résumé
Professional affiliations	Your career strategies
Cover letter	Associations that foster professional maturation
Résumé	Your major contribution
Cover letter-résumé	Main substance of package

Contact your nurses' associations for current professional information:

National League of Nursing
10 Columbus Circle
New York, NY 10019

American Nurses Association
2420 Pershing Road
Kansas City, MO 64908

Chapter VI

Nursing News Update

New nursing challenges are emerging continually. Fascinating medical technological advances and exciting nursing specialty services are being developed to enhance your patient care. These challenges are welcomed and fostered to maturity by most nurses.

Today, however, another category of challenge is confronting professional nurses. These challenges probably have the impact and power to redefine the profession's very structure and parameters. What could these challenges be? Relying on your newly acquired nursing knowledge and your civics information, try to deduce them. (Hint: One is a fatal disease.) Your reply should include:

- AIDS (acquired immune deficiency syndrome).
- Severe nursing shortage.
- Liability insurance.

Let us examine these three highly visible challenges.

AIDS is a contagious, lethal disease. After a person has become infected with the AIDS virus, the body's immune system malfunctions, rendering it unable to fight off diseases.

Considering the definition of AIDS, how do you think this disease will affect the nursing profession in general and its individual members? These are the types of questions nurses are asking themselves and one another:

- Should AIDS victims be isolated on a specialty unit or in a specialty hospital?
- Would you, as a nurse, have reservations about rendering care to an AIDS victim?
- How would you react if you contracted AIDS from a patient or became a carrier of the disease and passed it to your spouse?
- Should the AIDS nurse receive higher pay and increased fringe

benefits (e.g., life insurance) because of the specialty training and increased risk?

The answers are emotionally charged, subjective in nature, and subject to change.

- Most professional nurses interviewed felt that AIDS patients should be treated with good precautionary techniques.
- Most of the nurses interviewed *would* render care to AIDS victims in accordance with specific guidelines.
- The question of contracting AIDS from a patient is highly personal, and other nurses' reactions should not alter yours.
- All nurses felt they deserved higher salaries and more comprehensive benefits for their services.

Just the whisper of the word AIDS sends waves of fear, hysteria, or panic through most people. What is being done to control this emotionally charged issue in the nursing profession?

- Guidelines for testing for the AIDS virus are being established at government and private levels.
- Procedures for patient care are being set forth and adapted.
- Nursing personnel are being advised of and inserviced in precautionary measures to prevent contracting the AIDS virus.

This challenge, although inherited by professional nurses, affects each of us directly or indirectly. Hence, public education is mandatory.

Currently, the nursing shortage is considered the most critical professional nursing problem.

- The lack of qualified personnel translates into compromised patient care.
- Without nurses, hospitals lose money. If there are not enough nurses to safely staff a unit, that unit must close (as dictated by the regulatory agencies). Every shift the unit remains empty is money lost. Hospitals must make a profit to survive.
- Nursing associations are allocating funds and developing national programs to alleviate the nursing shortage.
- Hospitals and other health agencies are offering incentive programs. A professional nurse who recruits another nurse receives a bonus (usually money). Nurses who will work a

specified number of hours per week are awarded additional financial recompense.

- Some health agencies are recruiting nurses directly from nursing school before graduation.
- Health agencies are participating in job fairs to advertise their expertise to the professional nurse.
- Nursing schools are striving to create programs to draw new nurses. Common components include greater flexibility in CLEPing courses, program hours, and financial assistance.

The bottom line is that nursing needs qualified professionals and will provide you with the assistance and guidance required to achieve your goal.

Let us look at the third issue that concerns professional nurses: liability insurance. Liability insurance protects a nurse's financial assets if sued for malpractice or negligence.

As the number of nurses decreases and the number of patients remains unchanged, overworked, understaffed nurses are at high risk for malpractice or negligence suits.

This constant state of high risk has caused insurance rates to skyrocket. The large number of suits has forced many insurance companies to cancel liability policies. Insurance companies, health care providers (nurses, doctors), health agencies, and even regulatory agencies are examining the problem.

What are the solutions to escalating liability insurance rates or the inability of professional nurses to purchase insurance?

- One emergency solution has been provided by a national nursing association, which provides liability insurance at affordable rates.
- Some levels of government are taking legislative action to resolve the issue.
- Health agencies and regulatory agencies have initiated stricter guidelines for nurses.

In spite of the AIDS scare, the nursing shortage, and the liability issue, nursing will thrive because of people like yourself with ideas, insight, intelligence, and interest in their profession and in mankind.

Index

people
  orientation, 3, 37
  skills, 31, 32-33, 69, 102, 112
perseverance, 35, 66
personality traits, nurse's, 31-
  33, 34-49, 66, 98
Personalized Marketing
  Packet, 91, 92
personnel inservice,
  coordinator, 80
philosophy, personal, 41, 92
position, finding, 89-124
Postpartum Unit, 22, 70-71
primary-care nursing, 6, 18, 87
prioritizing, 45-46
private duty nursing, 87
probation, 111, 120-121
Problem Oriented Recording
  (POR), 21
problem-solving, 32, 44-45, 80
procedure
  invasive, 22, 75
  radical, 84
professional affiliations, 99, 102
profits, hospital, 19
program, nursing, 50, 51, 52
  admission requirements, 54-
    55
  associate degree, 80
  LPN, 65
  pros and cons, 55-56
  work-study, 59, 60, 61
Psychiatric Unit, 22, 37, 39,
  68-69
psychological illness, 34, 69

Q

questions
  interview, 114, 114-116
  open-ended, 11, 42, 51-52, 97

R

reaction
  to accident, 28-30
  controlled, 70
  fast, 74
  intelligent, 33, 113
Recovery Room, 73-74
recruiter, nurse, 86, 126-127
Red Cross, 85
rehabilitation
  center, 85
  unit, 36, 39, 83
reports, patient-care, 15, 44-45
respirator, 33, 49
response
  appropriate, 113
  to ethical issues, 6-11
  impulsive, 32
  to patient, 3, 90
résumé, 93, 97, 98, 99, 108-
  109
  content chart, 107-108
reward, financial, 40, 67, 78, 90
  121
rounds
  assessment, 15
  patient, 44
  with physician, 15
rules, hospital, 15, 96

S

salary
  BS, 50, 68, 87
  increase for AIDS care, 125
  126
  requirements, 91-92
sales, medical, 87
SAT (Scholastic Aptitude
  Test), 53
satisfaction, of nursing, 3-4,
  27, 40

W